DAYS IN OLD SPAIN

Afternoon—Sahagún

GERTRUDE BONE

Days in Old Spain

ILLUSTRATIONS BY
MUIRHEAD BONE

London 1942
READERS UNION LTD
by arrangement with
MACMILLAN AND CO LTD

Made 1942 *in Great Britain*

PRINTED BY LOWE AND BRYDONE PRINTERS LTD LONDON NW10
PLATES PRINTED BY HARRISON AND SONS LTD LONDON WC2
AND PUBLISHED BY READERS UNION LTD
DUNHAM'S LANE LETCHWORTH HERTFORDSHIRE
AND CHANDOS PLACE CHARING CROSS WC2

CONTENTS

[v]

DAYS IN OLD SPAIN

CONTENTS

LIST OF PLATES

[ix]

Visigothic Kings mentioned in Text

LEOVIGILD (573–587). First Visigothic king whose crowned head appears on a coin. Greatest and most magnificent king of the Visigoths.

> *'The golden pome, the proud array,*
> *Of ermine, aureate vests and jewelry;*
> *With all which Leovigild for after kings*
> *Left, ostentatious of his power.'*
>
> SOUTHEY.

RECCARED (586–601). Son of Leovigild. Made a political conversion to Roman Catholicism of himself and court to bring about a more united Spanish people.

SISEBUT (612–621). Increased the territory under the Visigoths by conquering the Byzantine Province of the South-east.

RESCESWINDUS (649–672). His name is on the crown in the Louvre. Abolished laws prohibiting marriage of Spaniard and Goth. Forbade Roman Law: Romans and Goths alike being judged by the Visigothic Law-Book in his reign.

WAMBA (672–680). Defeated attacks by the Moslems on the eastern coast of Spain.

INTRODUCTION

It was once my purpose to write of and contrast two curious Spanish journeys five centuries apart in time, of which the aim and results were carefully set down by the travellers themselves. The early one, in the reign of Philip II, taken by the monk and scholar Ambrosio Morales, who journeyed by royal command to discover in what monastery or church was deposited the head of St. Lawrence (required by Philip for the chapel of the Escorial, then in building), and whose shrewd chronicle of his adventures gives one an idea of Spain in Tudor days such as one does not acquire from history-books;—and a latter-day journey taken in the days of the Dictatorship by Don Luis Bello, through the country schools of Spain, to record their number and equipment and to estimate their competence. This latter work, done with the zeal of the reformer and by no means with the placid acquiescence of the older historian, is, in the light of the present tragedy of Spanish civil war, of a pathos undreamt of by its dead author, as showing what reformers would be at long before the hammer of war felled that reformation on its own threshold.

Should one plan the contrast of journeys in these days through Spanish territory it would be with a heavy heart, to find much gone and more ruined that lay in the tranquil sunshine of summer and harvest, in the leisurely journeys which are the theme of this book. Oviedo? Naranco? Durango? the maize harvest with the flails, the wide-eaved Asturian houses—the church surviving from the Goths—they are like a harvest beaten by untimely hail. For now the Argentine proverb 'Let death come to me from Spain' can no longer raise a smile as at some incredible thing long delayed, but instead a shudder as at something imminent and menacing, so calamitous and swift is the death which reaps in the cities and corn fields of Spain. If it seems irrelevant in these days of Spanish war to recall the days of Spanish peace, perhaps it is only by the constant reminder of the fact (which in the statistics and offences of war is in danger of being forgotten) that the wide territories of Spain are full of beauty and a noble people, a people of affection and humour and of great fortitude and human dignity, that one can push aside the smoke of war for even a short hour and catch a glimpse again of that delectable country before it was rent and laid waste.

From the actual content of the book it will be evident that these impressions of Spain were gathered during leisurely visits extending over the last years of the old régime. The Dictatorship of Primo de Rivera, like a tottering wall, was leaning to its collapse. Disaffection to the Monarchy was everywhere audible and an impatience of backwardness and old fashions manifest in all parts of the country. With the passing of old customs picturesque history also recedes, and it is evident that even such recent scenes as are described in the present volume have been witnessed for the last time by the Spaniard himself.

The journeys in Spain taken by my husband and myself occupied months at various seasons of the year and in different districts of Spain over a number of years. They resulted in two folio volumes of important drawings by my husband, of which this small work is the text. The descriptions were written to accompany the drawings in the first place, and therefore only such subjects were chosen as could be presented pictorially. The diligence was still our method of travel, and it is worth noting that, with the arrival of motor traffic and a return to journeys by road, a throw-back of interest to places and scenes not touched by the railway has revived the importance of the guide-books by the traveller Richard Ford, and to some extent even of George Borrow.

From our wanderings in the Spains we have gathered both ripe and durable fruit. Its beauty is distant now and its people but a warmth of the heart, yet vivid, alive, enduring and heroic, they remain for us an experience and an affection which are Spain.

For permission to reprint two chapters in the book my thanks are due to the Editor of the *Manchester Guardian*. Some short historical foot-notes are supplied for the convenience of readers who are not familiar with Spain and its history.

Chapter One

RONDA—ZÁHARA—
GRAZALEMA

RONDA

'When I named the countries of the West, he enquired if there were not Moslemín living in some of them. I told him that long ago a rabble of Moghrebies had invaded and possessed themselves of the florid country of Andalûs—Andalusîa was a glorious province of Islam. The Arabian plant grew in the Titanic soil of Europe to more excellent temper and stature, and there were many bulbul voices among them, in that land of the setting sun gladdened with the genial vine. Yet the Arabs decayed in the fruition of that golden soil, and the robust nephews of them whom their forefathers had dispossessed, descending from the mountains, reconquered their own country. As I said this, "Wellah *guwiyîn! then they must be a strong people"* answered Amm Mohammed.'—c. DOUGHTY.

Andalusia is so easily accessible from Gibraltar that perhaps the mountain town of Ronda gives many travellers their first completely Spanish sensation.

After the mobile distances of blue water for four days, sunlight again strikes heat from warm soil and light from whitewashed houses, and a circle of grave Sierras stands waiting what skies and colour and shadows the winds bring to them.

Looking over the edge of the gorge on which the town is built, which still keeps the mould of whatever stupendous and fiery upheaval once happened in the heart of those mountains, across the wide circular valley like the crater of a volcano (wide to walk across on foot and deep to look down into, but narrowed to a parterre of cultivated greens and ambers, when the eye looks across to the peaks of the Sierras and sees the scale upon which the mountains design)—peering down upon the vultures hovering in the valley, the flocks of kestrels and hooded crows, appearing even more numerous because of their shadows on the sunlit soil; and then to San Cristóbal and the belt of pines which grows only at a certain altitude;— one takes one's first knowledge of the clarity of air and sunlight which contracts the distances and depths of Spanish landscape. For distance and space are qualities which the imagination must set itself to absorb in this country. 'League' is a word which has greater expression in the Spanish landscape than 'mile', the latter being a word too reminiscent of measurement and ordered roads to convey adequately the spaciousness and expanse of sky and country which must become familiar to receptive eyes.

There is little opening out of distances, however, for the

[2]

train which climbs the 2000 feet from Algeciras to Ronda. But if it is springtime and the hill slopes are lighted with yellow broom and the sunrise renews every morning the living white beauty of the cistus petals, if a desert railway cutting is blue with the tiny Spanish iris, and valerian and peonies and oleanders make the shadows radiant, one forgets the suspicion of facile romance which echoes in names, in the enchantment of one's approach to Spain through the real beauty and colour of fertile Andalusia.

One takes account of the habits of sunlight very soon in Southern Spain, where shadow is hoarded in the streets and in the churches, and where old men follow the shade for their rest as in England they follow the sunshine. One can watch colour become negligible at the solstice and see a little shingle-roofed town be lost altogether on the hillside as the sunlight asserts its habit of drawing all the colour to itself at midday. On the tawny earth of the highways of Southern Spain black has all the value of a colour. Nowhere, perhaps, does one appreciate the black sombrero of the men and the mantilla and black dress of the women as in this southern province. Legacy from the veiled Moorish women, or of convent habit, it is wonderfully right, out of doors in the sunlight. Even the ilex groves and the cork oaks take a silver glitter at midday. Only the shadows of the buildings yield nothing of their gravity, and the black head-dress alone retains its outline.

It was, indeed, in following the habits of the sunlight at Ronda that I had my first contact with the simplicity and courtesy of the country Spaniard, and the doors of his country opened to me, as it were, by a charming gesture. All the world loves an artist at work. For one thing, he can be placed, and his business in the country understood, when that of the tourist bewilders the simple. The reserve of the Spaniard is never surly. He requires his own personal dignity, but he will invariably allow you yours. If he knows what will please you, and you are a well-behaved person, he will of his own accord open an entrance to the interests you seek in his country.

There were certain elderly gentlemen who took their morning walk within the public alameda. It was also my habit to write there, and after observation of the habits of trees and their shadows, to go at a certain hour to the fragrant dusk of a pergola heavy with roses and lilac blooms. Here the shade remained all morning, and here I was joined by the elderly group who sat gravely exchanging the small-talk of the town.

It happened that one morning I was at work upon a poem, and the irregular appearance of the lines upon the page drew the attention of one of the gentlemen to my occupation. He observed in an undertone to one of his friends that I was a poet. The gentlemen looked around. From beneath the gentle shadow of trailing petals the Judas-trees in monarch's purple could be seen and the sunlight caressed the hollows of the Sierras. 'A fit place for a poet to write!' said the gentleman with satisfaction.

'Very truly, a fit place!' agreed the others.

Every morning we exchanged our salutations, when one morning a younger man joined the group, preparing to sit upon the bench which I occupied. He was at once interrupted. 'Do not sit upon that bench', prevented one of the gentlemen in an undertone; 'you may disturb the rhythm.' The young man glanced, raised his hat and seated himself elsewhere. He evidently considered it reasonable. And one evening when I was sitting on the edge of the gorge as the sun was going down an elderly man in a cloak in whom I recognized one of my morning group seated himself near me. My back was towards the mountains. The old gentleman rose and approached me. He removed his hat and entreated me to look round. All these things happening in the heavens and a poet sitting unobservant? I rose. He waved his arm to the splendours. Poet—sunset! Sunset—poet! The introduction was made. I directed my smiles and my appreciation to the sunset and my bows to my dignified old friend. He was gratified by my appreciation and I no less by his simplicity and the charming way in which, understanding my habits and my pleasures, he had wished me to lose no moment of that which I had come to his country to seek.

ZÁHARA

Sunlight and scents of earth and springing growths, blue borders of iris along the dusty roadsides, naked boulders of mountains and the silver of eucalyptus-trees high overhead and fragrant; the languor and stillness of midday over the corn fields, and a town cut out of air as it were on the ridge of a spur of the Sierra; the whole population ranged along the town wall to watch our approach and a great part of it staying with us for the day, forsaking us only when we left the town at sundown; so we found Záhara, a Moorish town on a bridle-road which girdled the high peaks of the Sierra del Pinar in the days of the Moorish occupation.

What is left of the citadel of the Moors may at this moment as well be Provençal as anything else, for all that remains. Situation and outpost of Moorish intelligence once, Záhara is now a small Spanish town going about its own affairs, sufficiently unvisited by English or foreign tourists to make the arrival of a party a matter for the whole day's interest. Whether it is a delusion of the eye it would be difficult to say, but one always seems to be walking along ledges in Spain. Towns are built on mountainsides. Roads lead round shoulders of hills. And whereas in Scotland one always seems to be entering and making one's way up a glen, in Spain, wherever one looks, the outline of mountains is laterally placed and one never seems to be making one's way between them.

Záhara especially seems lodged like a high-built ship whose inhabitants look over the side to hail a passing vessel. As with a newspaper from home after a long interval in a foreign country one has a feeling that it should really contain some news important as its rarity, and then one finds it full of affairs of small-talk already stale and over-breathed; so one climbs to a little hill town unused to visitors and finds— women washing at the fountains, little girls coming from school at dinnertime, and beside each a small case with a tiny bit of white sewing (along the hem pricks of blood), an arithmetic-table book, and a catechism—a man gathering a swarm of bees—the plaza lying waiting for shadows—the shops darkened from sun—donkeys standing by doorways with panniers of produce—a blind convent wall keeping its secret—the chill of shadow by the church (mass all over for the day), its treasures brought out tentatively in the sacristy —some coloured tiles built into its belfry, and the sinking away of ground from its isolation into tilled country and high-roads and the affairs of towns and men, with corn-lands surging up to the base of its rock like a sea, as variable as the sea in surface, though coloured by the earth.

GRAZALEMA

On the Moorish hill road, flat on the hillside like a city of tombs, lies Grazalema at the height of 4000 feet, linked to

Záhara by the ancient mountain bridle-way of the Sierra del Pinar, which travels round the spur of the mountains and never sinks to the valley, where one comes back to something of the earth's heat among the boulders and waterless peaks of San Cristóbal. Up here, untouched by caprice of weather, are plants which have left the variable conditions of lower latitudes to unfold and live happily in high summits. The banks of gum cistus and pale broom make a shining highway for the sunlight of early morning in the valley. Hanging on the boulders, like flame bursting, are masses of yellow biscutella. Rare flowers for the botanist make the crevices rich.

Grazalema is like a long street climbing endlessly up from its gate to the mountain peaks beyond. Little boys are setting hollow tubes to catch the 'Gri' Real' which is chirping loudly all over the mountainside. The little cages in which they keep them are like the toys sold at English fairs or hung on Christmas trees. But the eyes of the botanist are to the hills, the home of the *Abies Pinsapo*, for above Grazalema is the last place in Europe to be favoured of these pine-trees. Vultures circle with the slow ease of the mighty and out-of-reach. Naked rocks radiate heat and seem accessible in the purity of the light into which they thrust up their heads, and up here the pines have made a seclusion for themselves.

'Once', said the innkeeper, 'some men came and tried to take away the pine-trees. But shortly afterwards the men died. It is not lucky to touch or interfere with those trees.'

When reindeers wandered over Europe and the great forests softened all outlines and blurred distances the *Abies Pinsapo* grew farther north. Now it survives only in Europe in the mountains of Grazalema, an Atlas race still holding a territory in Spain!

Chapter Two

SEVILLE AND CADIZ

PORT OF SEVILLE

'*There came a Paket as of letters inrolled in a seare clothe so well made that thei might passe to any part, beeyng never so farre, the whiche beeyng opened, I founde a small cheste made of a little peece of Corke, of a good thicknesse sette together, whiche was worthie to be seen, and in the holownesse of it came the hearbes, and the seedes that the Letter speaketh of, everythyng written what it was, and in one side of the Corke in a hollowe place there came three Bezaar stones cloased with a Parchement and with waxe in good order. The Letter was written with verie smalle Letters and sumwhat harde to reade. . . .*

'*As in this Citie of Sevill which is the Porte and Skale of all Occidental Indias, wee doe knowe of thē more, than in any other*

[8]

partes of all Spaine, for because that all thynges come first hither, where with better relation and greater experience it is knowen. . . .

'*And other thynges, whiche now are brought unto us in greate aboundaunce, that is to saie, Golde, Silver, Pearles, Emeraldes, Turkeses and other fine stones of greate value, yet greate is the excesse and quantitie that hath come and every daie doeth come and in especiallie of Golde and Silver. That it is a thyng of admiration that the greate number of Milleons whiche hath come besides the greate quantitie of Pearles, hath filled the whole worlde: also thei doe bryng from that partes Popingaies, Greffons, Apes, Lions, Gerfaucons and other kindes of Hawkes, Tigers Wolle, Cotton Wolle, Grain to die colours withall, Hides, sugars, Copper Brasill, the Woode Ebana, Anill. And of all these, there is so greate quantitie that there cometh every yere, one hundred shippes laden thereof, that it is a greate thynge and an incredle riches.'* — Physician NICOLAS MONARDES, of Seville, 1569, quoted from Miss ELEANOR ROHDE'S *Old English Herbals.*

Against the daffodil sky of a December sunset, the fronds of the tropical palms in the Plaza of San Fernando move like the state fans of an emperor. The rows of orange-trees growing in the streets are decorated with ripe fruit. A water-seller is still seated by the foot of a tree, her clay pitchers and vases in a pyramid beneath its shade. On the quayside beneath the Golden Tower, groups of seafaring men, pilots, and small skippers sit at tables in the open air, drinking beer and eating olives and shrimps. The wharf is lined with timber and pig-lead. Donkeys, small in stature but resplendent in ornament, pass in train, carrying stone and sand for the highways and buildings of the great exhibition now numbered among the historical monuments. It is the port of Seville, whose history is housed in the Archives of the Indies. In a narrow corner near the Alcázar is the house given to Admiral Bonifaz, who forced the sea entrances and broke the bridge of boats by which the Moors defended Seville from the sea. 'ESTA CASA FUÉ CEDIDA POR EL SANTO REY D. FERNANDO III Á SU ALMIRANTE D. RAMÓN BONIFAZ, CUANDO CONQUISTÓ Á SEVILLA, LIBER-TÁNDOLA DEL DOMINIO SARRACENO.' In the Biblioteca Colombina are the pathetic relics of Columbus, first ruler of the Indies.

It was the sea which gave Seville its surest defences, yet it was by sea that she was taken. By sea also—the wider Occidental Ocean—that she rose to her renown and became tribunal of the Indies, and it may be this outward-looking attitude, this consciousness of contact and access to a new continent, which fixed her status long ago. Reviewing the other provincial towns of Spain, Seville, next to Madrid, keeps the poise and liberality of a capital, though the high-way of Columbus is now traversed only by small barques and coasting steamers, while iron girders and the concrete blocks of modern engineering clamp the Triana to the side of Seville where the Moorish bridge of boats was broken by the Admiral of San Vicente.

A town with the aspirations of a modern capital begins to display a certain ruthlessness towards antiquity. Half-Oriental Seville, with its carelessness of street fronts, its once blind façades broken into at a bad building age, has now arrived at a period of town-planning, when streets must be more than alley-ways to reach a postern, when vistas are considered of consequence, and a house-owner has a sense of the city to which he belongs.

But even when strange cargoes and stranger merchants unloaded from the Indies beneath the Golden Tower, there was a time of ambitious building. For the construction of its mighty cathedral, 'planned so that men would say its builders were mad', must have occupied almost all the lifetime of Columbus. Each landfall he made must have found it further advanced, each departure with some new development in progress. Seville without its cathedral, its ancient mosques still in place and with streets as close and secret as Córdoba, would be the Seville whose image Columbus first carried to the Indies, and to whose quays came every year one hundred ships.

The pleasure of the Arab town, so silent, so unassailed by traffic, lingers with the scents of its myrtle hedges in the lanes at the back of the Alcázar gardens, the style of living a modified form of the Oriental, the shining of the interior courts flashing green plants and palms and the glitter of fountains on the wayfarer. And where there are no natural elevations, where the wind travels along a river from the sea, and the climate ripens oranges, there must be gardens, and here Seville is beautiful. In the winning sunlight of spring, roses cover the gardens like a cloud. Arches and walls of cypress, hedges of myrtle and jasmine, send up sweet scents even to a December sunshine. Conceits and pretty devices (formal as a book of hours with coloured margins), water used as deftly as silver threads to hold dropping lights, mysteries of obscure green walls and mazes, fill the gardens of the Alcázar. This is Seville of the Moorish picture-books.

The Moorish architecture of the Giralda tower, lovely and sweet-coloured though it is, has impressed Seville too much. Smaller Giraldas alone seem possible to later builders. But one is bound to be impressed and exalted by Seville's great Gothic church. One wonders to see such height, such space, such solemnity, until one comes to its centre. The five mighty aisles of the cathedral contain the sanctuary as a flaming heart. Magnificence needs the gloom, and the greatest piece of gilded Gothic carving in Spain shines like a trophy of the gold of the Americas brought so long ago by an hundred ships a year.

There is something a little depressing in the fact that Arabian splendours can be so easily imitated. That given certain lights, a tea-shop in the Moorish manner looks very little different from the boudoir built in the Alcázar by Pedro the Cruel for his mistress María Padilla. The Renaissance combines more happily with Moorish decoration than the authentic architecture of the Moors, to my mind. Yet here and there in the palace of the luxurious Don Pedro, small and delicate columns have been used from the earlier palace of the Moors, and remain now with the stamp of that aristocrat among craftsmen, the Moorish stone-carver, like a gentle old patrician at a bull-fight.

Scattered about old Seville are the pleasant old church towers with rows of coloured tiles. Santa Ana, Santa Paula, with their enlivening strips of colour above the shabbier of the plazas, achieving a sort of friendliness with their surroundings, a cheeriness not out of keeping with street markets and the humbler kind of café and cinema.

The wide levels between Seville and the coast are cut into innumerable canals and waterways, with salt pyramids standing on the plain like studs pinned down upon a map. Yet another Spain has its mentality along the lowlands of the coast over whose marshes the Andalusian bulls roam in a sombre freedom, a Spain which does not look backwards but outward over the sea for the landfall of ships, and is concerned not so much with ceremonies and history as with enterprise and expansion.

The Spanish Bridge, Ronda

Court of Lions, Alhambra

Probably the small ships which now float down the Guadalquivir from Seville are larger than the actual ships of Columbus, which must have appeared above the fields much as the masts and sails of to-day. But it is to Cadiz near its mouth, shining from the sea as a white haven, that the big ships go now—Cadiz with its tropical palms and gardens and the sparkle of a lighthouse about it.

LOS PASOS

'Something a little grim about them?' I ventured tentatively after my first sight of the Pasos.

'Well: *wasn't* it a grim spectacle?' reproved my interlocutor with severe gravity. 'To me they are more religious than all the coloured and decorative processions of Italy. I am impressed by the pasos in a way which I never am by effects of banners and vestments. They appear to me to be truly religious in their idea!'

An attitude of understanding is necessary, then, before one can see with unprejudiced eyes. The Spaniard, whose temper is serious and simple, has also a certain literalness in his composition, having, in this matter of processions, its imaginative side. He has never chosen to refine the central act of Christianity to a tender poetry, nor the Figure which shook the world with its single arms to an appealing emblem. It is in this attitude one approaches the form in which his religious habit expresses itself.

All Spain awakes at Eastertime to a sense of religious festival. The Passion of Jesus is, as it were, re-acted all over the country. In some districts and towns the scenes are acted by the people of the town; the judgement on Jesus proclaimed from the balcony of the Ayuntamiento, the disciples,

[13]   B

the three Maries, the centurions and the Saviour, Saint Veronica and Saint John, walking to Calvary through the streets of their local town.

But for the most part the scenes are reconstructed by pasos, life-sized figures carved in wood, painted and grouped elaborately upon platforms which are carried on the shoulders of as many as forty men dressed in the habit of penitents. During the days of the Passion the processions reconstruct, as it were (among a people partially illiterate), the passage of Jesus through the streets and estranged populace to His trial, death, and burial. The carving of the figures themselves is of all degrees of elaboration, from the famous pasos of Seville, Valladolid, and Murcia, to the humble little local carvings of the villages. Sometimes the history of creation and pagan mythology are added to the story of Redemption. Sometimes the humble images of the village churches serve the purpose of the procession, which is the survival or re-newal of the old mystery plays of the Church, now, as in medieval England, in the hands of the trade-guilds of the town and followed in procession by the confraternities of these guilds in the distinctive dress of each order.

Seville and Madrid set the standards of magnificence, but it is always of Seville that one hears all through Spain. 'As in Seville', prints the tailor on his announcements for guild dresses. 'You have seen the pasos of Seville?' ask the people of the little towns.

So much a part of the town's life are these processions of the pasos that the sculpture of these wooden figures has attracted some of the best among Spanish sculptors and the pasos are not to be dismissed as merely popular and therefore inartistic. Montañés, Gregorio Hernández, Egas, Alonso Cano, Berruguete, Zarcillo, Mora, have all thought this a form of art worth attempting, from a single moving or tragic figure to a whole street scene; as in the pasos by Gregorio Hernández in Valladolid, which are often street encounters of his day, with quarrelling and rough gesture intended to make, as indeed they do, the scenes actual and vivid. The Lady Veronica, stepping outside her conventions, finds herself in the midst of a group of ruffians whom hitherto she has seen only from her litter. The scourging is carried on in a business-like way by soldiers tossing jokes equally lustily about a negro's striped trousers. The executioner shows no ceremony in the handling of Simon. Picaresque street scenes of his own day, very easily 'understood of the people'.

At times, when the streets are darkened at evening, when the pasos issue from the church in silence, save for the strange Oriental wailing of the *saetas* ('arrows' of song) which greet their appearance, when the penitents in grotesque black habits with lighted candles walk in two wavering lines, the skipping and jerking of their narrow trains on the pavements, the inclination of the peaked eyeless hood distributing strange shadows like bats in the moonlight, when the sculptured figures flickering in candlelight take a likeness to reality, the effect is moving and impressive. At times, even in the sunlight, I have watched the pasos take on the semblance of the actual scene.

As I was returning home in a little mountain town I was unexpectedly caught in a crowd which was waiting for the procession. Those in the rear of the advancing pasos saw an opportunity to intercept them by running behind the street buildings and emerging farther on. But the returning stream made progress impossible in the old Moorish street. The pasos were wedged in the crowd. The balconies were filled with spectators, and barely lifted above the heads of the people stood the figure of Christ mocked, hands tied, head drooping and wounded, torn garments, a roughly carved figure of some tragic intensity. Excited by the jostling crowd, a drunken gipsy began to sing a ribald song. The people, from rebukes, passed to jeering. Jests and protests were shouted from one to another. Suddenly an old woman whose fierce profile was cut, as it were, from her black shawl, began to sing a *saeta* of devotion in a piercing voice. The gipsy refused to stop and sang louder, taking it as a challenge. The people laughed aloud at both, and in the middle of the swaying, noisy crowd stood the tragic and abandoned figure, taking on in circumstance something of the fickleness and triviality which had brought about its Passion.

But this is the emotion broken about the pasos by accidental human lighting. There are, too, moments of dramatic intention. One day in a southern town I was in the plaza at the hour of the Crucifixion. Windless sunshine and the bright air of the mountains caught the crimson and purple of the guild dresses and gave them solidity and sumptuousness as the procession circled the plaza. The black mantillas and dresses of the women made darker the shadows of the heavy cornices and balconies. Suddenly a silence which was not of decorum fell on the crowd, and I noticed for the first time that the high blank wall to the side of the square held the great iron portal of the prison. As the suffering Christ drew near, the iron gates were flung open, the outstretched arms were lowered to pass under them, and He who gathered the souls whom men cast out passed into the prison. 'He was numbered among the malefactors.' It was a great gesture and the only religious one of the day. The crowd dispersed in silence.

LAS SAETAS

As the groups of the Passion are carried through the towns and villages of Spain during Holy Week, short, flying songs greet them, supplying the dramatic reaction to the sculptured tragedy enacted in silence along the highway. To watch the spectacle of the processions and not to understand these songs, these *saetas* which greet and accompany them, is to go away with only an imperfect appreciation of the most popular religious festival in Spain. One knows how the mystery plays in England arose from the singing of the Passion in the churches, became elaborated, first within the churches and then outside, until abuses caused them to be suppressed within the Church, only to be taken up by the trade-guilds, to be performed and staged, sometimes as tableaux and again as acted parts, until they in their turn gave way to the less popular 'Moralities'. And just as one reads in old records how the 'Pessoners and Mariners' were responsible for the staging of Noah's Ark and the Flood, the bakers for the Last Supper, the carpenters for the Crucifixion, etc., so now in Spain, where the intention of the mystery plays has survived in the form of life-sized sculptured groups of figures carried on platforms through the streets in Passion week, the craft and trade-guilds of each town make themselves responsible each for one group.

All traffic being stopped in the streets on Thursday until Sunday is past, the pasos repeat the incidents of the Passion in their due order and at the recorded hours, and the action and speech, as it were, are supplied by these 'arrows' of song, launched apparently into the air by the spontaneous feeling of the crowd in the street. Part expressions of devotion, part wake-songs or dirges, part survivals of acted scenes, intoned on high notes with a strangely Oriental music, the effect of these 'dark grieving doves' circling the head of the Crucified, of the mourners and of the Lady of Sorrows, naïve and rude as these sometimes are in execution, can be deeply moving in their effect.

An admirable collection of the *saetas* of Andalusia has been made by Señor Agustín Aguilar y Tejera, with examples of characteristic music. It is from this collection I quote some *saetas* which seem to me to show their dramatic origin; but any young girl will sing a *saeta* for one, in the South, and the fact that there are so many of them and so well known to the women shows of itself how deeply this popular expression of religious feeling holds the imagination of the Spanish people. One is to think of the darkened streets at midnight with the Paschal moon riding the clouds. The long black lines of waiting figures, the Cross with all the world's sorrow upon it, lit by the candles of the penitents in black hoods, advancing upon the night, cleaving the dark with its light like an opportunity. Suddenly upon the darkness flies a *saeta* to greet it:

> *Lift up your eyes on high!*
> *Tell out with all your powers*
> *The thing which Jesus suffered*
> *In His grievous passion.*

or, more dramatic:

> *'They are striking blows on Calvary.*
> *Magdalene, what does it mean?'*
> *'Ah, it is Jesus of Nazareth*
> *Whom they are nailing there.'*

or again in swift action:

> *Who will lend me a ladder*
> *That I may climb the Cross*
> *And draw the nails from the hands*
> *Of my Father Jesus?*

or like a funeral dirge or wake-song:

> *It is so narrow a bed*
> *They have made for the King of Kings,*
> *That He may not fall off it,*
> *He must set one foot on the other.*

Sometimes the *saeta* is like the short chorus to the drama:

> *In the street of bitterness*
> *Mother and Son encounter.*
> *The Son raises the Cross,*
> *But the Mother bears its grief.*

> *'Where are you going, Mother,*
> *With such grievous mourning?'*
> *'I am going to see my joy*
> *Which is left on the Holy hill*
> *In its last agony.'*

There are *saetas* for every development of the tragedy;
for the betrayal and judgement, the supper, the scourging
and humiliation; for the disciples and mourning women,
and very many for the grief of the Lady of Sorrows who is
carried alone through the streets in the last procession. Some
of the latter are the most popular, and many of them poetic
and touching. The preoccupation of so many with the embroidered mantle suggests ideas reaching into folklore, but
to the women who send a *saeta* to greet the Virgin, the mantle
means the work of women and what they have been able to
afford for the Virgin's special hour.

There are no stars in the sky
Because all the stars
Have gathered in the hem of your mantle
To light up your sorrow.

Ah, Mary, you have been to heaven
And changed your blue mantle
For one that is black
For the burial of your Son.

The tears of the Virgin
Fall trickling down her mantle.
They shine like flowers of the lily
In the light of the candles.

The pasos halt before the hospitals and there is one *saeta* quoted by Señor Aguilar which I cannot refrain from repeating, though in a literal English translation it loses much of its pathetic intensity.

Open the window, Mother:
The Brotherhood is passing.
I am dying and I would see my Lord
Go to His last agony,
Oh! if I could die too when He does.

And for the prison:

Ah, Lonely One, give me your hand!
Here we are many brothers
without father or mother.

The processions have their interest as a spectacle, but the playing backwards and forwards of these *saetas* above their heads brings a deeper and more emotional quality into this festival, so popular among the Spanish people.

LOS SEISES

The long and learned history of the Seises of the Cathedral in Seville by Don Simón de la Rosa y López, sets the curious antique dance of the children before the Sacrament during the octaves of Corpus and Purísima, and the *triduo* of Carnaval, in a long line of liturgical ceremony.

The tradition of the processional dance is by no means obsolete in Spain. The Corpus procession at Barcelona is preceded by a group of little boys each with a ceremonial stick or baton which they strike as they dance, marking a beat in the music. In Santillana del Mar there is dancing before the altars in the street. In Compostela the cathedral 'giants' enter the cathedral with their pipers and dance in the sanctuary before the image of the Apostle Santiago. But the sacred dance as part of the highest ceremony of the Church survives now in Seville alone. The Seises dance at the most solemn moment of the church's festival, while the Cardinal-Archbishop, prelates and chapter kneel down to adore the Sacrament.

From the dancing of the early Christians, who, 'while they sang psalms and hymns in exaltation of the Deity, moved their feet, alternately advancing and receding, with expressive gestures of grief or joy'; from children who sang, to children who danced in procession before the Sacrament; from pageants in the church—David dancing before the ark; the children shouting Hosanna in Jerusalem; the company of angels at the Nativity—from ceremonies in the actual Cathedral of Seville like the enthronement of the boy-bishop, when a company of children dressed like angels were let down from above the sanctuary, and having enthroned

and robed the boy-bishop were drawn up again out of sight
—through all these changes the dance of the Seises has passed
in the course of centuries until it remained finally as it is
seen to-day.

There never were apparently *six* boys who danced. Los
Seises Cantorcicos were six children under ten years of age
who were introduced among the men in the choir to chant
certain responses for the effect of joyfulness which the children's voices produced—the name Seises being popularly
applied later to children set apart for certain offices; there
being actually, in the time of Philip II, sixteen children who
danced. Now there are ten.

The Book of the Seises in the cathedral archives discloses
elaborate rules for the education of the children by the
Master of the dancing and music, and their history much
bandying of discussion about propriety, and attempts by
the severer prelates to discountenance the dancing within
the cathedral itself. How the Seises used to be dressed as
angels—variations to the habit of pilgrims and shepherds
displeasing the people—and how the courtiers' dances of
the period finally set the costume in which the ten little
Spanish boys dance the antique dance of joy to this day,
are traced with much patience by their historian, who adds
that, be the origin what it may, the result is that the 'piety
of the Sevillians composed this picture of angels and set it
in the sanctuary of their sumptuous basilica, to give testi-
mony to all time of the intimate communication of heaven
and earth, art and inspiration'.

In December, when church ceremonies are not crowded
with foreign sightseers, the dance of the Seises in honour
of the Sacrament is placed in the chief festival of the Virgin
—La Purísima Concepción. Ten boys in the costume of

pages (possibly of Philip II's reign), in the blue and white colours of Mary, dance after Lauds in the sanctuary of Seville Cathedral. What is it like? A very slow folk-dance, paced rather than danced. A dance of eight set figures, making, it is probable, a sort of liturgical hieroglyphy, danced with no semblance of passion or movement of the arms, save for the occasional beat of the castanets—a pacing and swaying to the singing of the boys themselves, the time being punctuated by the pulse of the castanet, this grave rhythmic pacing and twining before the altar, tracing symbols on the floor, conveys to the onlooker all the significance of a rite.

The figures of the dance are quite set. Each figure is danced to the time-compass of separate verses, quicker or slower as the music suggests, and each figure must finish with the verse. The quicker movements 'do not alter the serenity of the dance since the dancers, to supply the *leaping* in the dance, raise themselves simultaneously on the tips of their toes, and mark thus the beat of the chant, the result being a kind of step very accentuated and uniform, having nothing in it resembling the leaping of the profane dance'.

The dance occurs in the afternoon at the public exposition of the Sacrament. The pillars of the nave and aisles are hung with sixteenth-century ruby velvet of Córdoba. The silver altar is burnished, the pulpits hung with the blue and silver of the Virgin. A towering silver monstrance holds the Host above the altar. The figure of La Purísima stands between those of her two great defenders,[1] San Leandro and San Isidoro. Behind all, the gilded Gothic *retablo* (reredos) rises

---

[1] The brothers St. Isidore (Archbishop of Seville) and St. Leander defended the doctrine of the Immaculate Conception. St. Leander was persecuted by the Gothic King Leovigild and fled to Constantinople. Various Eastern features of the early Spanish Church are said to owe their origin to Leander's acquaintance with the Eastern ritual.

to the Rood high overhead. Two benches covered with carmine velvet enclose a space about four yards long by three in width in front of the altar. 'After Lauds, the chapter, preceded by the cardinal, issue from the choir and solemnly remove to the sanctuary, all prostrating themselves before the Holy Sacrament, near those who are about to dance. The chapter intones the Tantum Ergo, and at the conclusion the ten children appear on foot between the two benches, one in front of the other in two lines, each with his hat under his arm and his hands provided with castanets.'

There is a ceremonious kneeling by the children to the Sacrament, and an equally ceremonious donning of the blue satin hat with its white plume before the dance begins. If one bears in mind that the cardinal and prelates and chapter kneel during the whole duration of the dance, and rise only to take more openly the position of adoration on the steps of the altar, one realizes how intentionally the dance is part of a solemnity.

The figures may be, and probably are, of symbolic significance. The significance of the ground cross and the double cross is evident; the double SS for Santísimo Sacramento; the I for IESV. The circle with boys outside may be the Host guarded by four angels. The circling of ranks of angels in the twining may or may not be symbolized. Who shall say how this antique rite, which from the costumes of the boys *might* be Opera, has turned out to be religion? What line divides—as it certainly *is* divided—this dance of the Seises from a folk-dance on an English lawn?

My habit of lingering after ceremonies led me now to see an unpremeditated effect above the altar. The cardinal and the dignitaries had gone and the congregation strayed vaguely to other altars of the Virgin.

Now between the intricate stage of blazing candles, great wax columns erected on steps, tiny rings of tapers, white and comely and holding flaming blossoms, long white wings began to climb. In a moment two serious rosy faces appeared between the candles, two childish mouths pursed like cherubs of the winds. It was only two choristers blowing out the lights, the long hanging sleeves of their surplices drooping like floating wings, yet angels stealing in to put things tidy could have looked no prettier; nor early Italian sculptor conceived any theme more joyful.

LA CRUZ DE MAYO

It may be soon among the forgotten customs, since it has been forbidden this year (1928) as offering opportunity for the meeting of conspirators. If, in the month of May, when the Swedes dance in their villages round a maypole with garlands and crowns, and the English with ribbons, you were walking down a street in Seville and noticed over the door a green bough, you would know that within the patio of that house there would be a *cruz de mayo* (May-cross). The nailing of the bough above the door is an invitation, and if you are curious or interested you may knock on the door and ask to see the cross, remaining if the family and neighbours dance round it, and leaving a contribution as you go out if the family are of the poorer sort.

We found our Cruz de Mayo in a large tenement house which had once been a convent. The doors were discreet enough, but nothing could have been less like a convent than the interior. The usual square patio with three arcaded corridors one above the other had its ornaments and carvings defaced, but the dignity of a beautiful Renaissance building was still visible under the decorations which fluttered from every pillar and were festooned across the patio. Paper streamers, tags of lace curtains, sashes, and old fans, made an astonishing flutter and bravado, and from every crevice and aperture suddenly appeared more children than one would have thought the whole street contained. On the old convent well-head, in the centre of the patio, stood a cross of green. At the sight of us, girls and young women ran here and there for their *mantones*—cheap little silk squares with fringes. Without these apparently the dance was not beautiful, or was, at any rate, incomplete. A young mother with a baby threw both baby and apron into the lap of an older woman and took her *mantón* from a little sister who had run to fetch it. Everything was very improvised, very spontaneous, very merry, and good-natured. What young men there were took their places as a band of musicians below the cross. No castanets being available, it was their function to keep the measure of the dance by snapping their fingers and beating their palms. The little boys sat in a precarious pyramid on the well-head watching to see how we liked it.

It was impossible *not* to like it, this bolero which the women had danced from childhood, so graceful, so dignified, so rhythmic even without the sound of music; this swaying and passing and linking of bodies without ever touching and to the order of some harmony running through each movement. It was as if a wind had controlled the mobile limbs of the women, so unconsciously, so simply did they respond to the dance and the beating of time.

'Did you like it? Did you like it?' The children and girls crowded round to ask. Happy, informal, kindly. 'Yes!' we had liked more than the dance.

Chapter Three

GRANADA: I

THE KINGDOM OF GRANADA

If one enters the Kingdom of Granada where Boabdil left it, though the shimmering of the green strath glances before one, it is neither its fertility nor its prosperity which surprises one first, but the superbness of the spectacle lying out under the sunlight. As truly as in Zion, one's eyes are towards the hills. For the snow-line of the Sierra Nevada lifts its authority above the Vega, and one knows, even before one reaches Granada, that the seat of sovereignty will be there.

If it is springtime and the drifts of blossoming trees throw the fairness of a veil over the early green of the Vega, such a thrilling of life is within it that it becomes, not colour staining the ground, or watered maize fields, but a living thing captive within the silver network thrown by the snows, beautiful and breathing.

Certain words from an older phraseology creep out of hiding, 'Fastnesses', 'Living Green'. Within the splendours of the Sierras would seem a security hardly to be questioned. On cloudless days the clear sun lowers heights, and the mountains offer themselves, magnificently accessible. But draw closer, the rushing and exhilaration of the silences among those naked peaks slashed by the sunlight, their myriad inaccessibilities, the seclusion of the passes, make the foothills seem fragile in substance and their tender green cultivation faintly exotic beneath the exulting age and seclusion of the great cloud-battered summits. Surely a fastness? And yet! If it is autumn, one sinks deep into the fertile Vega, weighted with crops and stirring with labour. The small wheat harvest is but an interlude in the green abundance of maize and sugar beet. Everywhere the rippling of the irrigation channels through the responsive verdure is like the passing of a sweet wind.

Here and there reapers are cutting the corn in patches with sickles, and the horses are treading it out on cleared spaces. It is not the serious epic land of Castile in harvest. Yet the flaxen dust blown from the winnowing heaps gleams pallid in the green luxuriance. Stubble is whipped by fire, orange, red, *solid* almost in the ineffable light of the evening. Crops grow round the very walls of the farms, set unenclosed upon the land. *Ventas* and *posadas* by the wayside are busy with beasts and men.

A whole population is at work in the classic beauty of the fields which shine in the long golden evening of Spain. From below, in the heart of that coloured and teeming lushness, the mountains rise, arid, violet, African. In one mile of the Vega one has travelled many, so varied is the surface, so narrowly crop folds on crop. The roads are full of movement—herds of cows followed by their calves in patriarchal march—goats going to milking, swine rooting in bean fodder. The crops, weighty and deep, hide the harvesters. Along the roads between the harvests go the carriers and mules and oxen. Long wagons piled high rest at the wayside *posadas*. One thinks of the actual *weight* of the produce lifted from that thirty miles of a double-yielding cultivation, and then of that grim advance across the Vega, beating down, burning, destroying, and at the end that little tablet in the tower of the Vela within the Alhambra: 'This day the Catholic Kings entered Granada'.

Fortress towns in the mountains 'above the clouds and the swallows', orchards and corn fields in the watered valleys, the ten-years conquest of Granada is the warfare of these two. Surprises, forays, and loot in the valley. Siege and destroying engines at the walls of the towns. Like old Scottish Border warfare, often carried on like a private quarrel without presence or immediate cognizance of the sovereign.

They were the days of gesture, behaviour, of pageant and set pieces whether of mockery or grace. Doughty deeds, achievement of arms, war with the Saracen, an open path to glory. Did not the Douglas bear the heart of Bruce with the circumstance and retinue of a King across Flanders to the Kingdom of Granada, that in death his King might join the war against the Infidel which was denied him in life? 'Press where thou wert ever wont, dear friend.' One is stirred yet by the flinging of the heart of Bruce to the front of the battle, though the battle is written in the smoke of the clouds. 'That he should wear these on every anniversary of this day' was Ferdinand's royal gesture, taking off his robes and dispatching them on the instant to the Marquis of Cadiz for a gallant defence. Glory is in the doing, not the reward. Did not the Greeks run for a wreath of parsley?

Yet there was attrition and wearing down and cruelty, destruction and harassing of overseas commerce and of the development of the country's natural resources. The siege of Ronda, the capture of Záhara, the battle for Alhama, the fall of Granada—ten years and Spain belonged to the Spaniard.

'One *must* always become a little silly if one begins to imagine the Moors back in the Alhambra!' said a wise young Spaniard to me. Yet even in the Alhambra one gentle Moorish dominance persists. The coolness of the hillside nights receives the vibrations of a bell in the tower of the Vela to signal the opening and shutting of the water-sluices upon which the fertility of the Vega depends.

The little dusty town of Santa Fé lies out among the maize fields of the Vega of Granada, where two men settled the future destiny of Spain. If Boabdil and Columbus ever actually met face to face, might not the Moorish King have warned the explorer, 'Better is he that putteth off the harness than he that putteth it on!' But the Arabian learning had lifted the eyes of Spain to horizons. It was in a sense the age of geographers and travel. Spain ruled as far as Naples. Mathematics, astronomy, geography, had settled as sciences. Merchant venturers came from the East bringing 'ivory, apes, and peacocks'. The possibility of undiscovered countries had been demonstrated unanswerably by the private expeditions of Prince Henry of Portugal. Frontiers were mobile and the business of the founding of kingdoms very active. Trade routes and pilgrimage ways were open and travelled. Isabella's system of government was like that of a wise mother alert for every opportunity of expansion and growth. More dramatic than the capitulation of the citadel of Granada was the overtaking in the Vega of a bitter man riding away on a donkey with the weight and torment of a discredited vision in his heart, and his slow return to the town of Santa Fé to take his sailing orders from the sovereign whose sagacity was alert only just in time. Columbus, Ruler of the Indies, started his tragic and difficult destiny from the plain of Granada. Heavier than his last days of neglect and poverty would be the knowledge, one thinks, of later years, of the retreat of his dead body carried once in honour from Spain to Havana, removed thence to Santo Domingo, and at last carried home to Seville for burial, marking thus in death the outposts not now of conquest but of relinquishment, Ruler of the Indies no more.

'Let me be buried in Granada. Let me lie next to my lord and husband', said Isabella's will. Side by side in the royal chapel, before the carved *retablo* which records the history of Granada's conquest and the fulfilling of her heart's desire, within the magnificent *reja* (grille) placed there by Charles V to honour the 'little place with so much grandeur', lie the marble effigies of the Catholic Kings; and here, once a year, Granada celebrates the day of her faith and independence. Across the silence of the crowded cathedral the silver trumpets sound three blasts and a voice cries aloud the cry with which the Catholic Kings entered Granada in the year 1492: *Granada! Granada! Granada! Por los ínclitos Reyes Católicos Don Fernando V de Aragón y Doña Isabel I de Castilla! Viva España! Viva El Rey! Viva Granada!*

> *How the voice cries there, calling alone in the silence!*
> *Under the rigid stone does Isabella hear it?*

THE POMEGRANATE

'I will pick out the seeds of this pomegranate one by one', the speech of Ferdinand is reputed to have run, and to-day there is Spanish 'Granada' (pomegranate). A town within the resplendent vibrations of the eternal snows must always keep about it some hovering refinement, some atmosphere a little keen and unusual. Perhaps this is the reason why, on the slopes of something so near perpetuity as the Sierra Nevada, the late Moorish architecture of the Alhambra looks a little gimcrack. Except for the genius of situation the palaces of the Moorish Kings look better on the level, or rising amid gardens. Elaboration of delicate ornament does not disguise poverty of architectural structure. That the escape of the eye from the windows across the wide country is the finest gift of each room seems one's first disappointing knowledge. Then a detail of beauty will draw one apart;—the delicate blondness of the colour in the courts, gracious as sun-warmed ivory or an old faded fan; the grace of the clustered pillars in the Court of the Lions, the proportion and state of the Hall of the Ambassadors, and one knows the Moors for the wonderful craftsmen they were.

A shell without lustre? Fountains without water? Lamp unlit? Is this what the Alhambra remains, emptied of the state of the Moorish Kings? It may be so. Colour revives colour, and the halls of the ambassadors and kings, the gardens of women, are now a stage scenery to which there are no fit entrances or exits. Certain inventions of pleasure send echoes. 'The Moors knew how to live!' says the attendant of the perfumed baths and the galleries of musicians. Sounds of fountains, fragrance of gardens, spacious courts of shadowed sunlight, where tragedy walks in fancy dress, remain. The great shimmering of green on the Alhambra hill still shelters (though repute credits the planting of the trees to the Duke of Wellington) one of the Moorish tendernesses, the singing birds, and the nightingales in the gardens of the summer palace make the sunlight an enchantment. How the Moors used water too, playing with it, festooning it, working it like precious metal or diadems in the radiance of the sunlight! The cypress avenue in the Generalife leads to beauties of lyrical waters. But what remains is not interesting as the mosque at Córdoba is interesting. Something already a little on the decline and weakened seems to cling about the palace of the Alhambra. One is somehow not sorry that the Moorish dominion ended. In Córdoba one feels a strong and vigorous culture, rising through apt and pliant channels and not hostile to the civilization within which it is flowing; the presence there also of a race more capable than that amid which it is expanding. In Granada it is the unstable position of a race between arms and luxury, having already lost the solidarity of unity and ready to be ousted, a little purposeless too, having nothing but magnificence to express. The skin of the pomegranate was already gaping. Its seeds were ripe to fall.

'One must always become a little silly if one imagines the Moors back in the Alhambra.' But not, I think, if one were to imagine them in the Albaicín (Moorish quarter), or the bazaar in the town, or the old tannery which tradition says Lope de Rueda[1] used as a theatre. Perhaps the merchant is less operatic than the Sultan and more credible, having

[1] Lope de Rueda, the Spanish dramatist who revived and regenerated the Spanish theatre, died in 1565.

continued longer into our own day. In the Albaicín—that crowded town—high whitewashed walls with narrow steep ways lead suddenly to a blind plaza with a latticed window and one green tree. There are ways whose straitness admits no vehicle and where one must stand against the wall to let the strings of donkeys go by. Streets and plazas have the air of something not secret, but not disclosed. The eyeless streets (with windows looking inward) are at once populous and furtive. The arch of the 'needle's eye' in the town wall lets through its beasts of burden and their packs with difficulty.

It is easier to grow lyrical about the oleanders which the Moors never planted, however beautiful they are, than to convey to oneself the richness of the deposit which must have been left on the hills opposed to the Alhambra. Sculptured by men, handled and modelled for centuries, these hill tops now are as eloquent of civilization as buildings themselves could be. The gardens and summer palaces which once covered them as the Generalife does to the present, have left something as definite on the olive-laden slopes as a patch of tilled and abandoned downland. The walk beneath the Generalife beside the Darro, on the ledge trodden for water every evening by women and children, to the Fuente del Avellano, gives, as no recounting of splendours can do, the impress which the Moorish civilization left on the territory of Granada.

JUNE EVENING; SIERRA NEVADA

It is like an old fresco or some wonderfully composed and tinted missal of ancient Christian art, in that it refuses to accept any object which cannot be mingled in its magic.

The sky is as soft in its blue as a new-fallen snow field. The stars are a tender diaper enriching this blue, dim and frail, disentangled now from the daylight in which they have been hidden. The mountains are covered with bloom like a late fruit, that veiled jewel-blooming with which the east wind surrounds them—blue and grey as moonstones, soft as cinnabar, glowing as topaz. The snow is insubstantial as streaks of moonlight. No great snow-glories now! The snow, shrinking and climbing higher, is like fugitive star-light. Near at hand the olives in orderly docility are enveloped one by one in leaves and silence. The aloes hold silver blades. Between them are wide moon-laid spaces of earth. But these are beautiful of themselves. Now the cane chair is absorbed and is transformed to a chair of ivory. The clumsy stumps of the balustrade are like kneeling silver elephants. The atmosphere, like the substance of an old fresco, absorbs all violences of tone: every colour, every shape is in a magical alembic. For an hour the enchantment is sustained. Then the moon, surging through the element, blinds all the little stars and holds the heavens like an eternity, white, without any flaw.

Chapter Four

GRANADA: II

'THE DANCE OF THE LIGHT'

Where the foothills of the Sierra Nevada taper out in long descending plateaux scoured by savage ravines, so narrow that from a distance their declivities look like roots which hold the mountains fast to the Vega from which they ascend to their snows, there are hidden away strange townships. Who would think that the smooth knoll over which the snow-airs from the Sierra blow clean and clear is in reality a village of caves in which a whole population lives as in a hive, whose chimneys and doors appear at your feet as you follow goat-tracks through the prickly pears which lift their clumsy Caliban flippers as you pass among them! It is a scorched and slippery hillside they cover in the summer solstice, and a violet light on ash-coloured summits irradiates an African-tinctured Spain.

From the top of the ridge of the *barranco* (gully) one can see into the caves on the other side, and, morning after morning, from a ledge half-way up the wall of the hillside, the sound of tapping comes up the ravine from a black-smith's forge in one of the caves. The tiny flame of the forge flickers across the distance like a candle in a dark lantern. The blacksmith moves about his work, a bending and rising shadow. He is a blacksmith, but he is also a *gitano* (gipsy); he is moreover an *old* gipsy who dances the 'dance of the light'.

It is a matter of some irritation to the Spaniard that the 'voluptuous dances of the gitanos have such a fascination for the foreign tourist', and the commercialized and impudent aspect of the gipsy dances arranged for the sightseer might well disconcert the sensitive. *But* a blacksmith *and* a gipsy who danced a dance called the 'dance of the light' seemed other and irresistible! We would make an attempt to see him.

Down a narrow dipping lane which precipitates itself with its stepping-stones between the flowering aloes like a snake seeking its hole, in the evening we paid our first visit to the smithy. The death-flowers of the aloes rose twenty feet high, erect and angular from their octopus-armoured roots, on both sides of the gully which is the King's highway of the cave-dwellers, straight to the ledge on which the blacksmith's smithy is lodged. It is only a black hood of rock over the forge, and the forge a cabin of flat stones with two bellows such as used to hang in farm kitchens in England. The flame is not out, but the blacksmith is. His little girl, a tiny sprite, elfin, un-Spanish and chattering, blows the bellows for us lest we should have come for nothing. Her father is not there. We adopt the solution so ready to hand in Spain. 'Mañana.' We will come back to-morrow.

'To-morrow' we re-travel the track between the lines of aloes. Again the blacksmith is out, but his wife is there to attend to us. 'The dance of the light.' Yes, her husband dances it. It is 'muy gracioso'. If that is what we want he will come up the *barranco* himself in the evening and arrange it. We 'go with God', and re-climb the *barranco*.

At sundown, as we sit out of doors, 'El gitano', announces the little country girl and now we see our blacksmith—a wheedling lovable old gipsy, slight and graceful as a youth. He will dance for us in the cave on the ledge in the evening. He must get the guitar, a girl to clap her hands, another girl to dance the dance with him, and a little wine, for 'one leaps better when happiness is in one's head. May your honours go with God!' and all the next morning we can see the gipsy's wife sweeping and cleaning out the cave from the opposite side of the *barranco*.

An evening of splendour dwindles narrowly above our heads as we climb down at last to see the 'dance of the light'. The neighbours are standing round the cave. They have hospitably brought extra chairs, but they do not come in with us. The cave is cool in the evening and spick and span with emptiness. It is a scooped-out rounded cavity such as a child makes in a sand-hill, whitewashed inside, a rack of shelves with plates and cups hanging in the prominent light of the doorway, a coloured picture of the Virgin of Cova-donga above it, and a row of rush-seated chairs round the wall. The gipsy has brought his two daughters. The evening light comes in from the door. We seat ourselves with cere-monious wishings of health and the protection of God. We bow over wine we are offered but leave it to the gitanos to

[38]

drink. They drink from a bowl one after the other, a sort of grace-cup. We are waiting, it seems, for the guitar. In a moment it appears in the arms of a gipsy-boy who sidles a little sheepishly into the dark corner of the cave. Quite suddenly he strikes the strings, and an unexpected sonority of sound fills the cave. The music finds its way to a rhythm. 'Anda-a-a! Anda-a-a!' call the gipsy girls sharply with a long wailing intonation, and then, with the whirlwind of the guitar music and that strange clapping of palms together yet out of the rhythm, which can never be left out of these dances, the dance of the light began.

The blacksmith folded half a newspaper into a rigid rod and, tucking it into his trouser-band behind, made a short stiff tail. He threw his hands above his head and snapping his fingers he leapt, singing in a monotone which rose to a shout, a mesmeric repetition. 'Now I am going to dance— I dance—Jota-a-a—Jota-a-a!'

'Anda-a-a! Anda-a-a!' wailed the girls.

He advances gracefully with little skipping steps, balancing, bending, leaping, with a backward turning of his head as if attentive to the tail behind. With a stealthy continuous movement of his body as he skipped and turned he kept the stiff tail swaying. From the side of the cave stole his daughter, bending almost double and advancing in a slow sinuous motion with arms stretched far in front of her holding a primitive open lamp like the earthen lamps on the graves in the catacombs—a lighted flame like a tongue at the tip. Soon they were together. Sinuous and stealthy and dangerous the meagre body of the girl, agile and bewilderingly alive the vivid grace of the man.

'Anda-a-a! Anda-a-a!' shouted the women.

'Jota-a-a! Jota-a-a!' chanted the man. The girl was near

[39]

enough to set the light to the tail. With a leap and a writhing, the tail had flicked out the light, and the dancer was off again leaping and skipping little goat-steps, the tail more active than ever.

The crouching figure of the girl crept out again, her lamp relit. Graceful, balancing, arms thrown high, he danced all round the cave, now more animated, pleased, and excited by danger. 'Jota-a-a! Jota-a-a!' 'Anda-a-a! Anda-a-a!' The crying is incessant. Again the light is flicked out and the girl slinks back to the shadow. Now he will tempt her! He takes no more steps. His body is balanced upright on his quivering feet, his hands with curling fingers are graceful and high above his head, and only by a quick movement of the hips which keeps the tail alive does he seem aware of the music and the beating of hands. The extended arm steals out with the light and the creeping body of the girl follows as a swimmer follows his side-stroke. The girl's narrow feet keep time in tripping steps.—This time she has him! 'Anda-a-a! Anda-a-a!' wail the women.—The gitano's body seems to be poised on wire, but he balances without advancing, his feet, his hips, his tail alone quivering to the time. She swoops low in triumph and the lighted flame is busy among the folded papers. Like an angry wasp the tail attacks it. To one side and then another the flame is beaten. The slim body is quivering from head to foot. 'Anda-a-a! Anda-a-a!' 'Jota-a-a! Jota-a-a!' A leap, a flick.—The light is out.—A whirl, a leap, a cry, and the gitano is on one knee on the floor, the end of the tail safe beneath him, and the girl bows solitary over her extinguished lamp. The gitano drinks our health and wants to know if we like it.

Where did he learn it? Very, very far away from here! No other gipsy knows how to dance it in this *barranco*. It is a dance of great antiquity he believes, but no one dances it here. It is *muy gracioso*, shall we do it again? The first time he ever danced it was at Gibraltar, and never once has the tail been set alight.

They dance it again, the stealthy girl from the shadow, the skipping joyful man. I am temperamentally averse to the great god Pan. When I see his name printed I sniff warily, suspicious of silliness and vapouring to follow. But, those skipping goat-steps—that mischievous naughty joy? No! they dance it again and it is more like the grace of Etruscan figures circling an antique vase. Has the light or significance now gone from the dance? When the little boys in Spain gather dried roots from the hill, and, lighting bonfires, leap through and over them on the day of San Juan, they do not know that what is left for them to do in fun their grown-up ancestors did in worshipful earnest to herald the summer solstice. The flicker of ancient ceremonial fires dances in every race. In the dark little cave and in the *barranco* for a moment or two the dance of the light seemed to take on such a flicker. Then there emerged another quality—of merriment and good manners in the middle of poverty, and a gipsy-wife smiling proudly at the accomplishments of her husband.

EL SANATORIO PURÍSIMA CONCEPCIÓN

From the cool patio with its fountain and palms and the shade of its drawn velarium, a dim tunnel of vines runs down to the garden wall, outside which a country road travels far below. Heavenly blue convolvulus drops its living azure down the withered branches of the peach tree. Oleanders fill the shadow with the still rose of a primitive picture. An old cypress gives gravity to the wall. The light green canes round the tank of gold-fish shimmer like the reflection of the water, green as a copper mirror in a marble frame. Ancient ce ar and eucalyptus-trees hold their kindly roof at a cool height and detain the sound of the wind. The palm-tree is full of unexplained agitations. Stone benches of an antique simplicity show grey and lilac in the reflected light of the yew arbour. Myrtle and box borders enclose late-blooming roses. From the terrace on the wall which guards the leisurely aloofness of the garden one looks across the Vega into the full heart of the orchards, deep green, hiding white farms. All day pack mules and wagons raise a dust in the road outside the garden, and men and women weed and hoe in the orchards or the fields of young maize, full of activity. But on the terrace or in the shadowy garden lie those whom an old religious phraseology used to speak of as 'laid aside'—sick men and women enduring the perplexities of their suffering. Carmelite sisters in their brown habits go backwards and forwards, quiet, vigilant, kind.

'No people in the world', wrote George Borrow of the Spaniard, 'exhibit a juster feeling of what is due to the dignity of human nature, or better understand the behaviour which it behoves a man to adopt towards a fellow being', and it is just when one is beginning to have doubts of one's own human dignity, a quality so difficult to disentangle from the earthen vessel in which it is enclosed, that the little Carmelite sisters reassure one.

I am in the garden in the evening. The sisters are decorating the convent for Sunday. The flowers they are arranging seem beautiful to me, but Sister Virginia comes from the province of Valencia where 'there are many many flowers. There are flowers in Orihuela even in winter.' The flowers of Andalusia seem so small, so poor.

The Mother is searching about among the flowers. Presently she comes to me with a bouquet, blue agapanthus, scarlet gladiolus, white marguerite. A slight air of something more than meets the eye comes with her. Ah! red, white, and blue! The English colours! I have understood, and at thanks more fluent than my Castilian a ripple of laughter runs round the patio.

An enlivening smell of burning rosemary comes from the kitchen. Encarna is beginning to prepare the dinner. She sits in the middle of her kitchen at her marble table, a vivid and tiny figure, white cotton dress, white stockings, noiseless white *alpargatas* (rope-shoes). Her withered brown face with faded and kind black eyes is wrapped round with its white kerchief, her ears swinging two enormous gold moons as ear-rings. The kitchen is white too, tiled, with porcelain stoves and white-tiled floor. Scarlet saucepans and casseroles line the shelves and walls, as merry as it can be made. To watch food being prepared at those tables is to watch the delicacy and precision of a surgical operation. Round the galleries go the sisters carrying trays of *alimento* (nourishment) to the patients from the white kitchen with scarlet saucepans. There is no hurry, no ejaculation, no hustle. In every movement they have the repose of those who seek no farther.

By and by Pilar nudges my elbow in the dining-room. I am only half helping myself it seems. If I dig deep down into the soup I shall find cockles at the bottom. 'Que se come!' says Pilar at last, and heaps my plate herself. The Mother adopts a cheerful outward philosophy towards her patients, whatever her inward religious intention. It is, in substance, that you may be all the fine fellow you think yourself to be, but if you have no health she would like to know what on earth is the good of you! One exclamation escapes her as trouble after trouble comes in from the world outside: 'Jesús! qué mundo!' ('Jesus, what a world!'), but it is obviously her vocation to repair the damage. The efficiency and quietness and happiness of the sanatorium are the adequate speech of religion.

Sister Virginia is our nurse. I become the 'lady of the *pabellones*' (balconies); my husband, 'the sick one'. 'Como está, enfermo?' ('How are you, sick one?') asks one gentle voice after another as the sisters go about their work. We learn from them how to manage the heat of a Spanish house in the summer— how to leave that heavenly invention, the Moorish water-jar, on the balcony through the cool night. We run out to see the garden irrigated every eighth day. We count the strokes of the bell which the portress rings to tell which doctor has arrived. On the instant house-surgeon and orderlies appear in their white coats. Sister Virginia stands vigilant. Order and quiet are great aids to recovery. We get well!

The Spanish doctor has no bedside manner beyond the Spanish dignity. Just a kind man come to see you through a difficulty. Dr. Sangrado died many years ago in Spain. Don Antonio Rodríguez, I set down your name with thanks as a *médico* of tact, of kindness and great efficiency. We talk in the garden now to the patients and learn their history. From time to time the wailing of a poor crazed girl whose lover has repudiated her, sobs through the gardens. 'Enrique! Enrique! come back to me!' Sister Faith passes quietly to the operating theatre. Paco and Joaquín are lifting stretchers from their shed. There will be an operation in the morning. There is a well-equipped theatre in the sanatorium. To-day it is a peasant from the hills who drags a poisoned leg. He

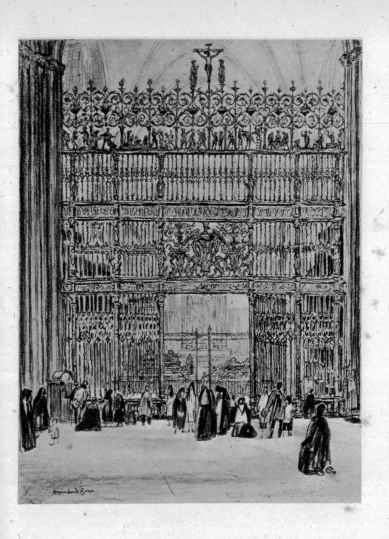

The Tomb of Isabella, Granada

The Cathedral, Valladolid

talks to no one. There is a sort of puzzled hurt in his eyes, strained and sleepless. Downstairs in the patio two old peasants in their best black clothes wait in silence, motionless, save that now and then the old woman wipes her eyes with a large clean handkerchief. Paco and Joaquín carry a burden past my door. Sister Cándida runs down smiling. It is all well over.

I notice quietly that praise is repeated but not blame. When the evening is breathed upon by a wind we all wander in the garden together, sisters, servants, patients, talking with the easy democratic intercourse of Spain.

The efficiency of an English hospital is magnificent but it is apt to bristle. The band of professional decorum is easily slipped. The simplicity of the Christian profession applied to every part of life is a blessed thing to encounter if one has fallen by the wayside.

The little waiting maids in their white overalls are playing hide and seek among the oleanders. 'Ah! Spanish girls! Spanish girls! You cannot find anything better!' sentimentalizes a youth, turning his head to a friend lying beside him.

We ask Sister Faith about the Duke of Wellington; she replies, so that we shall not be hurt, since he is a countryman of ours, that the Sisters being nuns do not read the daily papers and so do not know of current events. They question in their turn.

Sister Euphrosyne is surprised to hear that England is an island and is reached by ship. America? Yes! The journeys of Colón (Columbus) are well known: but—at this point let the Scot turn aside his ears from hearing vanity—Sister Perpetua had always understood that Scotland was the capital of England.

DAYS IN OLD SPAIN

Sister Virginia looks up the Spanish word for a gentleman's pyjamas with much laughter from us all. Attended by Pilar I go out to buy them. My return is that of one safe home from strange perils. In such a life the smallest things interest, the greatest are not overweighty, since things are great or small only within some greater and overshadowing idea.

Courteous old Spanish house, gentle women, farewell! We were strangers and you took us in. We were sick and you cared for us.

BACKGROUND OF GOYA

Something unusual is coming up the road to the cemetery. Four or five times a day the death-tray is carried past my lodging. One always knows a funeral by the chattering of voices long before it comes into sight. But it is something strange which is approaching. Its strangeness makes itself felt like a voice. Four little boys are carrying a tiny open box covered with pink muslin. Within, its pathos softened with flowers, is gathered as short a life. A boy behind carries the lid of the baby's coffin. Its black cross covers his breast. He is only just remembering not to sing. It is such a familiar happening that there is no effort to grieve made by the children. But now there follows a strange grotesque line of mourners—a straggling, uncertain, groping advancing of men—each with his face searching upward, each with his hand on the shoulder of the man before him. *All the procession is blind* save for a man who leads them up the mountain road. 'Et lux perpetua luceat ei.' Around is a superb panorama of mountain and sunlight, and stumbling on the slope are children carrying a dead baby, and a funeral procession of the blind.

Chapter Five

CASTILE

Its soil searched and crumbled by the sun, this land of hard beauty is like the passion for righteousness in a religious heart; once it has been felt, nothing softer, nothing less arduous contents one. It is the centre of Spain too, and its spirit.

Yet Castile is as various as many Castiles. There are vine-lands and walled cities, as well as the stark corn-lands and pueblos. Cuenca is of Castile as well as Salamanca, Toledo as well as Aguilar; and while the heat of June is in Madrid, shepherd and sheep may die of cold in the 'cradles' of the Sierras de Gredos. Crossing the vine country, one is in a shallow sea of viridian with white wine-presses shining in the green, gleaming up suddenly like white waves on infinite water; simpler in its elements than the corn-lands, not entertaining, as they do, the varieties of sun-shadows and tones. It is the cloud reflections which hide here, and ruffle the green, glancing back from its surface as from blue and swaying water.

The endless undulations give the charm and variety of Castile even as they vary the crop. On the Meseta are smaller table-lands scoured with rain and snow channels and gashed as savagely by the sunlight, and at times one's passage through the Guadarramas could only be expressed by Old Crome's picture of the Slate Quarry.

For a time in spring, when Castile is as green as the Eildon Hills and the wind whirs and sings over its great spaces, the horizon seems to be ruled with a ruler, an endless rim with light behind. Farmers with their cloaks flying, ride with an Arabian ease about their fields. Something of arrogance is in the demeanour of the Castilian *charro* (farmer), as of a person who knows no master but the sun. It is this Castile of castles and corn-lands and pueblos which has the compelling and stern beauty of Spain. If one crosses the great granary floor of autumn, with flaxen dust of grain enveloping the threshing *eras* in golden glory, the atmosphere itself seems to have changed to some opaque glittering, like the heart of a dimmed sun. Every town becomes a farmstead, every harvest group an allegory of labour lit celestially. Peering through the halo one sees the labour itself, sun-smitten, lean, enduring. The sun is here a conqueror. Children are there and women, oxen and mules and men, all moving to command. The sheaves are reaped with sickles, and the threshing-floors are as the Romans left them. The corn thrown, unbound from the sheaf, in circular spaces of flattened earth, waits the threshing. Upon it is driven a heavy wooden sledge, its underside teased with nails. A rope yokes it to the necks of two oxen, the body of a young charioteer weighs it close to the grain. Round and round goes the progression of the team, pressing the ears, treading and kneading the corn. Then the women come with long rakes gathering the straw from the shed grain. Girls and children follow with wide forks of wood, and from the heaps of tossed and winnowed wheat stream those golden smokes which signal all over the lands, of harvest gathered and ripe. Silvery shadowless heaps of grain stand in the moonlight like tents of a beleaguering army. Here and there the cone of dark, which is the watchman's hut of pine boughs, is vivid as an emerald in a pale setting.

Over the lands, sometimes on a long visible road, sometimes dipping behind an undulation as behind a wave, travel the long wagons piled with sacks of corn. At the stations— wayside halts—they are stacked, waiting removal, and the plain between village and village has the clean blond emptiness of a stubble field, an emptiness in which a high-piled wagon acquires the importance of a castle. At the stations, too, groups of harvesters with thick blankets, their sickles bound with straw and slung round their necks like bugles, sit on their bundles ready to follow the harvest. In steep places the mules and donkeys carry the sheaves on their backs, and once a procession of girls bearing sheaves on their heads made an antique ritual about a humble *era*.

This morning I am attentive to my roll of bread—'Bread of San Isidro, made of flour selected from the best wheat grown in the five towns'. Now and again there breaks to the sight that tortured, twisted, and left-alone landscape, frequent in Spain, gaunt and abandoned save for flocks of goats and sheep and the shepherds who live in its caves, ochre-coloured and forbidding. Sometimes plantations of umbrella pines, like some funeral pomp of woods, march in the distance. Everywhere the horizon is higher than you expect it to be. Gaunt, classic churches ride high on an undulation as on the crest of a wave, their western belfries of brick the first to catch the sunrise, the last to be illuminated in the sinking evening.

What a great outbreak of church building took place all over Castile in the seventeenth century! The high-shouldered brick churches of Castile rise and dip like ships amid the undulations. Every tiny pueblo has one of these high Renaissance churches, sad-coloured without, and of a dingy glory within. From the heavy bell-tower so characteristic of these lighthouses of the cornfields, the bells signal their sound, as if, behind the infinite extent of rolling country, the traveller might lose his way, as a swimmer bewildered amid waves. The bright green acacia-trees line up at the wayside halts, and motionless under their faint shade sits the human unit—young peasant, young wife, sleeping child. The old woman holding the signal baton is a familiar figure at the halts. Autumn is the season of the migration of the Estremaduran flocks to the lands of Castile. Slow dust-clouds rise on the highways, while the armies of long-legged trotting sheep storm the small towns on their passage northward, the shepherds and boys and dogs hot and hurried as the sheep. 'Ah . . . h! Come back there, wild beast of Portugal!' screams the shepherd, cracking prohibitions with his long whip fence about the flock. The torrent of sheep submerges the street. People crush into bastions on the bridges. The herd coming in for milking resent this scuttering about their evening harmonies. Later one sees the 'wild beasts of Portugal' feeding in the evening light, dusty, but unalarmed and tranquil in the unhurtful stubble.

CASTILE

A periodical came into my hands (lost before I could note the name of the writer). Its object was to set people right about Castile. Enough of this growing lyrical and spilling of poet's ink on the lands. Time the truth stood clear from this vapour of mysticism; Castile is the grey matter of the brain of Spain, generating intellectual heat—no poetry, nothing subjective, the merciless, the directing brain of its organism. Pure intellectual grey matter.

But poetry rides on the winds of Castile, and all the grey matter in Spain will not sweep it thence. Perhaps because it is of Spain itself that this land is talkative, that the poets catch fire. For, though there is much Spanish outside Castile, until you have seen 'las tierras onduladas' you have not known Spain.

MEDINA DEL CAMPO

It seems like a sorting station for all the affairs of Spain, which appear, if one lingers there in a hot August, to be whirled onwards with grain pollen and migrating sheep. Everyone sooner or later who travels in Spain must sit on that platform, where families of peasants seem to be established for ever, so invariable are their attitudes on their movable property, waiting for some train to come and take them to the end of the world.

Wandering outside into the quavering dim heat one feels that if someone hadn't thought of placing a castle there no one would have thought of putting a town there either. During the days of our stay in the *Villa* the big crazy Plaza was occupied by the tents of a menagerie, a fact which earned us, as possibly being connected with it, some measure of consideration. Above the flapping of tents, and the flocking of peasants, rose the roomy brick church, roof reaching after roof in higher leisureliness, as if to give in mass and spaces what it lacked in tradition and age. Is this church an appearance of the Flemish influence in Castile? With its high-ribbed vaulting painted white it looks like an unkempt version of Antwerp Cathedral. There is something, too, of Dutch light and cheerfulness within. The tower and bird-cage belfry with two homely wooden figures striking the hours seem as much for the markets as the offices, and indeed the Gothic and Romanesque churches never seem to fit into these animated market plazas as those of the Renaissance which Street calls 'pagan churches'. Flocks of living birds make an aviary of the open belfry, taking flight and circling over the Plaza at the striking of each bell.

Apart from the stir stands the high brick castle of Medina like a lighthouse in a dim-coloured sea, itself a frontier, it seems, against oblivion. How they planted those fortresses, winning back step by step of territory! How isolated they were! Looking from the top of the tower of Medina into the sad-coloured mists of midsummer heat is like watching for tidings from the end of the world. This August evening contains all the melancholy of Castile and its loneliness, in the fortress with its marvels of honeycomb and beehive brick chambers and its ancient resources of building. But modern history with a mind of its own chatters beneath it and goes on other highways. Isabella the Catholic died there. It can be seen from a great distance over the plain, mournful, sun-smitten, monumental.

Chapter Six

MADRIGAL OF THE HIGH TOWERS

MADRIGAL

The state roads cut across Castile give but an artificial idea of old communications between castles and villas, for the ancient ways lay like the loose string of a rosary on which villages were set as beads. Arévalo possessed an actual strategic position on a river with declivities. But Madrigal of the High Towers, set in a perfectly round disk, without any river, seems to have had no reason for its place on the chessboard of Castile, save that of apex to the triangle of Medina and Arévalo.

A town quite circular in plan, all contained within a wall upon which rose, at intervals of about forty feet, square towers with windows looking in every direction across the plain, Madrigal was entered by four singular gates. Three remain, with one uninterrupted line of towers. Two, like the broken apses of great churches with treble galleries of windows, dominate either side of the approaches by road. Within the walls peasants have built one-storied houses, whitewashed and decent, using the town rampart as the back wall of their cottage, like the dug-outs in the ruins of Ypres.

'More countrified than Arévalo', we were told we should find it. Yet the spacious ways of queens and *cortes* are still to be traced. A fine medieval hospital is in the lower plaza. The palace in which Isabella was born, with its quiet Alameda in front; the vast shell of a convent outside the walls where Fray Luis de León died; the broken house of King John II of Castile; the seignorial stamp on the houses rising to the Ayuntamiento; the size and bulk of Santo Domingo with its magnificent *artesonado*[1] ceiling, the *cortes* which sat here to decide successions to kingdoms—all declare an old important history. El Tostado, the learned grammarian, was born here, and his house is pointed out. But peasants of to-day will stop their carts and dispute whether that or this was the window from which El Pastelero (the Pastrycook) used to wave to Doña Ana of Austria in the convent, and which was the convent lattice from which she returned his signals. For Isabella may have been *born* in Madrigal, but El Pastelero was *hanged* there, and as the Alcalde said with a smile, 'If we have a play by Lope de Vega or Calderón the theatre will be empty, but let "El Pastelero de Madrigal" be announced and all the town flocks to pay its sixpences at the door'.

The Inn of the Star in the town of Madrigal of the High Towers must surely be the fittest place to hear for the first time the story of El Pastelero de Madrigal. Like the nursery rhymes which have survived all likeness to the lampoons which they once were, 'El Pastelero', like Guy Fawkes, would be difficult to eradicate from popular affections.

[1] Coffered and carved in the Moorish manner.

The Inn of the Star has a low wide entrance into a cobbled court and is in the lowlier part of the *villa*. Animals and men enter together. On one side is the *corral*, on the other the kitchen. On this cold winter day the kitchen hearth has a fire, half wood, half sawdust, and the dueñas of the inn sit around it watching the cooking of the earthenware pots which sit in the embers.

In the time of Philip II a certain priest, having fallen under his royal displeasure, was sent away to Madrigal, to an isolated promotion. Among other offices he became confessor to a convent of nuns in which Doña Ana of Austria, the daughter of Philip's illegitimate half-brother, Don Juan of Austria, was a nun, though against her will, she being cousin to Don Sebastián.

The death of Don Sebastián, heir to the Portuguese throne, was never believed by the populace. True he had last been reported in a desperate charge against the Moors, and had never been seen again, but the belief was deep in the story that he had vowed to go into retirement until he could wipe out the Moorish occupation from his country, and that he would appear again at the end of a certain period. Rumours would revive every now and again that he had reappeared. El Pastelero, whether prompted by the priest, or by his own vanity, announced himself as the missing Don Sebastián, her cousin, to the Lady Ana in the convent. She, being a lady of simple and innocent nature, believed in the spurious cousin—a man of unusual dignity and beauty of bearing— and they became betrothed—the priest promising to absolve her from her vows that she might marry 'Don Sebastián' and become Queen of Portugal, thus revenging himself on King Philip for his banishment and disgrace. Believing that Philip, her uncle, who had taken the crown of Portugal in the absence of the heir, had only to *hear* of the reappearance of the missing Sebastián to return the crown to him, Doña Ana gave her royal jewels to El Pastelero that he might sell them in Valladolid and get funds for the undertaking. El Pastelero, alas, had low habits as well as low birth, and took with him a woman of the town to Valladolid. To this woman he showed the jewels and she, becoming frightened, or suddenly jealous, told an official. The Alcalde came to inquire. El Pastelero was detained and the king informed that in his baggage were found letters addressed to 'Su Majestad'. The plot was discovered. The priest was deprived of such of his rights as were possible by a Catholic monarch. Doña Ana was deprived of her royal privileges and removed from Madrigal, protesting all the time that she was betrothed to her cousin Don Sebastián, heir to the throne of Portugal. El Pastelero was thrown into prison and sentenced to be hanged, drawn, and quartered.

It was now that this Perkin Warbeck of Castile began to play his part in the public eye, and, conscious of this, he played to convince. His bearing was that of a noble personage; his demeanour exalted; his attitude noble. His jailors were convinced that they had in their care the precious person of a royal line. He was induced to confess that he was not Don Sebastián, but held to the declaration that he was of royal blood and that if Philip really knew who he was he would not dare to condemn him to death. He suffered with fortitude, gratified that his Majesty, in the person of some small official, had at last recognized that he was a royal person and had sent some one befitting his rank to attend him to the scaffold.

'That's the window, Señores!' Two men dragged in their mules to tell me. 'Not changed—just as it was!'

'Look, Señores! Over there against the church wall he was hanged.'

'They say so', put in our guide parenthetically. But this could not be suffered. One might attack the church but not the pastrycook. We looked with sufficient respect at the tiny window of the medieval house and agreed that it could be seen from the lattice of the convent and that therefore one could almost see the pastrycook answering the signals of the princess from her convent. A rare hero of plays and romances, El Pastelero de Madrigal takes something the same place in the popular imagination as Robin Hood of Sherwood Forest or Dick Turpin, and Madrigal is proud of his possession. All in the round ring of its walls and towers, far away from a railway, Madrigal becomes more and more a village on the wide plain of Castile. The deed of gift of her royal allowance by Doña Ana to the convent, which is in the archives of the town, has a pathetic reality enough, but history, save for the gay Pastelero, grows shadowy there. The high towers crumble slowly. 'Fond of light wines' were the people of the town in the days when its importance was sufficient to be chronicled. Vines are few in the present day—for the vine is a touchy plant subject to diseases which do not visit the corn. We bend over the tomb of the Inquisitor —in the middle of the chapel floor—peer into the shadow of clausura to see royal tombs, pass again the grave and beautiful palace which saw the birth of Isabella and the seclusion of the bastard daughters of her Catholic husband, and the unhappy Doña Ana of Austria, and out into the freedom of the plain. No one will ever ride into Madrigal of the High Towers again and become important there. El Pastelero will be too much for them. He has been left in undisputed sovereignty too long.

Chapter Seven

ARÉVALO

KEY OF CASTILE

It is like casting anchor at sea to arrive at Arévalo at night with rolling moonlit billows of country retreating on every side. The express train draws up—The one passenger beside ourselves stoops and calls beneath it 'Ignacio!' and the country boy who never travels by any train, but who has acquired a familiarity with all as daily occurrences which drop an occasional item of business in his way, clambers through the carriage and alights on our platform. The inn, two miles away, to which he drives us, is an old palace, its long room looking over the town wall to an infinity haunted by the moon. To go out in the early morning is like going out on the deck of a steamer. The air stings. The peasants ride wrapped in plaids. This morning an important market of grain is being held, and the long plaza is lined on either side with the farmers' carts, painted brightly and in excellent condition, the yokes resting on the ground. A prosperous country one would judge from the well-set-up farmers and their families, and the handsome mules dancing sideways, the donkeys trotting like good children. Chestnuts are roasting. Paradors are crowded. From the walls one sees roads going everywhere like tracks on a chart. Watching a peasant clearing the first undulation, the only horseman on the plain, one wonders whether he will find his way or remain for ever, riding on to unattainable horizons. The hedged and walled roads of England look like permanent ways beside these open roads, which vacillate like the tired feet of travellers as they arrive at the town. Then daylight and sun disclose the stern uncompromising contours of Castile and its high bright colours: the ashen and orange fields of broad day; the economy of landscape as of islands beaten by sea and weather; the accent of black on tawny and bronze. A cart of green branches startles in the torrid road. The golden pennons of poplars pass below the city like those of a celestial host with banners, spare lines, black figures, golden tips, distant sierras flashing like blue steel, all the high lights of Spain pick out Arévalo on this late October day. Spare, hard, and kindly Castile lives on all round it, worked and trodden and levelled by centuries of harvest.

One of the strategic points of old historic Spain, the castle of Arévalo standing out in front of its town is planted like a bull, its feet embedded, as it were, and not to be dislodged from the formidable wedge of land it thrusts into the dividing river. For on the table-land of Castile, searched from every horizon, the points of defence and its surprises are not in elevations but in subsidences. Intaglio not relievo is the process which graved Castile.

Behind the castle, between it and the town, the bridges are carried across the two rivers which meet at its feet. Like formidable animals arising suddenly in the path, these castles of Castile, with their broken silhouettes still keeping the grand manner, have little advantage of situation. Only their watchfulness, their stubborn solidity, made them as islands of refuge in a wide sea palpitating with danger.

Within the triangle of fortified towns—Medina del Campo, Madrigal of the High Towers, and Arévalo—so near together, so full of the savour of Castile, rides the girlish figure of Isabella the Catholic. At Madrigal she was born—at Arévalo she passed her uneasy girlhood—at Medina she died.

Isabella riding to Arévalo in winter with the silver apple full of charcoal in her hands to keep her warm.

Isabella the small girl, with dim foreboding of her mother's sorrow and the dangers which hedge a queen.

Isabella in the convent of San Francisco.

Isabella with her little brother being taken away by their uncle, and the strange death of the boy.

Isabella the queen, riding with her gentlemen across the scorching plain to Arévalo to see her mother.—Two gentlemen dying of thirst, so that never after did she travel without a baggage mule carrying water.

Isabella forcing the illegitimate daughters of her husband into the convent at Madrigal.

This small area, these castles and convents, are full of the figure of the thoughtful girl with her private struggles and problems, beset with early dangers, who was to become the greatest force in Spain.

One scarcely knows Castile until one has lingered in its

smaller *villas*—Arévalo and Sahagún—Madrigal and Medina—Oropesa and Mansilla—the walled towns which one enters as harbours. One does not know the complete beauty of the land till one has watched the subtlety of autumn in the formidable grey of a Castilian north wind, when, in the withered rose and grey of the ancient bridge, a group of poplars and aspens shiver in the wind, living gold and silver—transcendent, incredible.

GÓMEZ-ROMÁN

In the church of the Bernardine nuns in Arévalo we read on the architrave between the church and the grille which encloses the convent, how two brothers (illustrious men), Gómez and Román, built a church in Lugarejo, but that, the times being unsafe for women, the nuns were moved to a palace within the walls, given to them by the emperor, Charles V.

Of whatever great building these brothers had built in the lonely site of Lugarejo, transept, lantern, and three apses alone remain, and from their situation, dominant and majestic, proclaim themselves from afar as treasure for the architect.

The Romanesque brick building of Castile is a study which develops fine enthusiasms in the Spanish architect. Differing from those which show the influences of foreign builders, the church of Gómez-Román is claimed as entirely Spanish and Christian and nobly independent of foreign or Mohammedan suggestions. Its grave and stately dexterity of building pleases even the artist. It is as if, set free from the conventions which govern stone, the builders took pleasure in their freedom, and explored with liberality the possibilities of their humbler material, working patterns in bare façades, herring-boning and diapering and fitting with great nicety their commonplace stuff to stately purposes of arcading and pyramid and lantern. No Mohammedan solutions of building, interesting as they might be, were attempted in this church of Christian Spain. 'The inspiration is Christian. The style and technique Romanesque-Byzantine.' Along a sandy road, two miles from Arévalo, one finds this lonely monument, on a rise by the side of the highway, like a mausoleum of great size, massive, dominant, and solitary; the most perfect specimen of Romanesque brickwork in Spain, to whose importance Señor Lampérez devotes a whole chapter. We climbed the knoll, slipping in the sand, on an afternoon of sunlight which lit a bitter upland wind. The washerwomen were kneeling at the river below. Goats browsed. Dogs barked. The pueblo was hardly more than a large farmyard with numbered stables. The threshing-floor, which had been against the church wall itself, still held its pale straw. Two gipsies rode up with us, easy and graceful on their donkeys. They bought a sack of flour at the farm, loaded it on a donkey, and, with all the children of the pueblo, followed us into the church. With much the expression of large dogs, looking first at our faces and then following our interest, as if to make out what all this was about and what we should get out of it, they sidled about at our sides. The interior domed apse and the placing of the interior brickwork—one wondered what they made of it, glancing from it to us with vacant bright eyes. Once outside, the eyes of both became wistful and melancholy, full of the sentiments which wheedle money from strangers. Receiving nothing, they both broke into loud laughter and rode away singing lustily.

The landscape became a harmony by Wouverman, with silver sand gleaming amid black tussocks of grass. The shepherd of the pueblo rode in from the fields, his cloak flying in the wind. Far away curved the cruel edge of the

Guadarramas, blue and sharp as an icicle. A voice spoke suddenly from behind. 'Who are you, Señor, and what are you doing here?' A donkey was almost eating the collar of the seated artist absorbed in his work. Bending over his neck was the watchman of the pueblo, a gratified smile on his face, since his soft approach had been successful.

'I am the watchman of this pueblo', he explained, throwing open his *capa* to show his brass badge. 'You are going back to Arévalo? Wait a moment and we will go with you.' Two men rode in from the country. The washerwomen lifted their heavy baskets and walked painfully up the loose sandy slope. Going to Arévalo takes more time than two miles would seem to warrant, for all along the way horses have to be collected and driven in before the men; conversation being thus interrupted and resumed to the ever-increased clatter of horses on the road.

'You are from England? It is a small country, is it not? Not so large as Spain?'

'But there are in London alone a third of all the people in Spain.'

'Caramba!' The dusk receives him. A trotting pony swings into company with the others.

'There are many Spaniards in London, you know—about five thousand.'

'Caramba! It seems there are more Spaniards in London than in the whole of Spain.'

'It is a great city, London! It has eight million people living there.'

'*Qué fantástico! Qué capital!* You have heard of Madrid? It is a Spanish capital. A fine city.'

'Spain has many fine cities. I have visited also Barcelona and Sevilla.'

'Spain has many fine cities, *un vasto terreno*, Señor. Go with God, your honour. This is our way. You go that way. With discretion, putting one foot before another, little by little, you will arrive.'

THE DAY OF THE DEAD
(November in Castile)

On this All Saints' Day the people are going, black travellers on a buff-coloured road, to adorn the graves of their dead. Below the abandoned castle, the plumes of the poplars glow orange in the low sunlight, throwing their oriflamme over the mortality of monarchs.

The late chrysanthemums and asters have now been cut in all the gardens where they have been keeping their bloom for this day.

On the hillside the cemetery has the tenderness of a garden, an oasis in the iron undulations of Castile, now grey under a north wind which uncovers prominent blue horizons, sharp and clear. All the town is at the cemetery. The road is good, lying along the slope of the hill. Slowly, all day long, companies have gone up this hill to visit and remember their dead. Servants carrying baskets of lamps, women and girls with flowers, children with moss and candles; all the population of the town is setting one way on this, 'the day of the dead'.

The cemetery is full of chatter and movement. Children run about busily, with full appreciation of this planting of moss and watering of flowers. Young men hammer into position the wooden crosses, aslant and forgotten throughout the year. Girls and women tie flowers in nosegays and light the lamps—many and splendid round the richer tombs, and, on the poorer ones, small tin lanterns swinging on the trans-beams of wooden and iron crosses. '*Tus padres no te olvidan.*' (Your parents do not forget you.) A cross of green moss brought from the river-bank lies on even the poorest grave. Here a few marigolds are sprinkled in the green—or branches of meadow ragwort. One beautiful tomb guarded by an alabaster angel is lighted by candles so thick that they flame like torches within their chains and boys warm their hands at the glare. Some of the graves are like the work a child makes on the sea-shore, mounds smoothed and patterned with heads of flowers. On some, the strewn flowers die with the day.

As the lamps prick the dusk a sudden illumination of the sky runs like a wave over the hill with the cemetery and the festival. Some lonely wandering ray suffuses it all with an intense and living glow. The poplars are lit like candles. The road becomes a golden street. Colour leaps the white walls of the cemetery and all save the cypresses flames. Nothing in the iron landscape is alight save this road with its ascending and descending groups and the quiet garden of the dead. So vivid, so intense is the beam with which the cemetery is flooded that the mourners look less real than the heavenly inundation. They move as blind people in the light. For a few moments it endures, illuminating the whole activity of human love and aspiration. Then it withdraws. The cold Castilian night appears as if at a summons. The candles flicker and lamps swing in a slow wind. The bells in the towers begin their counting of time by moments, as if to recall the living to the business of life. The people stream from the hill.

'*Tus padres no te olvidan.*'

Chapter Eight

VALLADOLID

THE IRON LILY

When Valladolid, that sunny and comfortable old capital of Spain, surrounded its court with workers in silver and gold, with sculptors and painters, and there was leisure to build richly—when the gold of America seemed enough to pave the streets of Spain and to take the place of golden streets of heaven in the Spanish imagination—who would have thought that it would in the end be the iron lily of Herrera which would be planted in so genial and prodigal a soil? The cathedral lifts its rebuke to trifling above the placid old town, which (court and kings gone long ago) has settled down to learn the ways of modern education and the solutions of modern building. It was Théophile Gautier whose soul loathed Herrera, who would thank God, as he passed through discomforts of travel in Spain, that, wherever he was and whatever enduring, at any rate he was not in the Escorial, and whose skin tingled with horror at the very imagination of this stone chastity. Fashion changes, and to every one comes his day! That of Herrera, as massive as the Great Pyramid and as rigid, is very much approved in modern Spain. His is not a style to be copied happily, for what in a great architect has solemnity, in a minor one is liable to be frigid and formal (as one sees occasionally in other churches of Spain). But, given Herrera, one can look for a grandeur of symmetry and conception.

Where did this soldier-born-turned-architect get his ideas? The severe neo-classic architectural style was not yet born, and nothing is more apparent in the architecture of the Renaissance elsewhere than a desire to please. St. Peter's and St. Paul's are both urbane in their intentions, suave in their appeal. But this pride which disdains to conciliate —which casts out ornament as a wind scourges the forest boughs, whence came it? Did Herrera, the soldier of Charles V, catch the prevalent spirit of world-empire, and finding it embodied in ancient Roman building reach that 'superbia' which bestrode a universe? Was there something in the fell temper of Philip which supported such an ambition?

We enter less than half the great design planned by the famous Spaniard. With the death of Philip and Herrera the east end of what is even now a very large church was formed by hastily blocking in the transept; the high altar being now placed where one would have entered the central space of his great dome. Even the fragment left of this superb conception is a mighty temple. So mutilated has the outside been, by the fall of one tower, which in its crash destroyed part of the cornice, by the bleakness of the granite of which it is built, which does not weather and is denied therefore the patina of old stone, that one is totally unprepared for the grave dignity of the interior. A few years ago one entered to be confronted by a boxed-in choir ludicrously out of keeping with the simplicity of the effect. Now, this year, 1928, a gust of Herrera has swept through the precincts. The *coro* (choir) has been cleared completely away, and stalls made from Herrera's original designs have been placed round the *capilla mayor* (high altar) itself. The wooden model of the cathedral shown in the sacristy as that intended by Herrera to be constructed is probably eighteenth-century, and does not correspond to the drawings of Herrera himself preserved in the Cathedral Library. These drawings (which the courtesy of the canons allowed us to examine) show a magnificent architectural conception. The high altar would have been on the eastern side of the domed central space, and behind it, unique among Spanish churches, would have been an immense choir facing to the west.

The simplicity and grandeur of the single order of the immense nave with its high cornice (a cart can drive along its width), above which the lunettes of a clerestory light the nave after the manner of a Roman tepidarium, moved even Street to a sense of awe (though he denied that it was religious). How much more had the building been completed! Surely then it would have been the finest classical interior of the Western world. Were it not for its grandeur of proportion and symmetry, justifying its ambitious challenge, the gloomy disdain of its patron would repel and oppress the spirit. But Philip was fortunate that he found an architect whose gestures outswept disdain, who could move with simplicity among austerities, who in the casting out of ornament substituted purity and nobility of proportion, whose symmetries satisfy like solemn music.

In the wooden model four corner towers are shown outside, but in Herrera's own drawings in the library it is evident that the eastern ones were intended to be carried up in a pyramidal form. Walking round outside the cathedral to-day one of the strangest architectural impressions is the appearance of the transepts as they emerge ruined and naked from the enclosing wall. There is nothing in the ruins of Rome itself which looks more majestic than this gaunt grandeur. A little farther on one sees the Gothic buildings to the east which were to have been swept away by the triumphant progress of Herrera's plan. In them the canons of to-day have their apartments and the drawings of Herrera are deposited. To crown this strange mound of architectural fantasies the late archbishop set up a colossal statue of Christ, which, flood-lighted from below, is grotesquely out of keeping with anything that stands for Herrera. But within, the gust of Herrera blowing through the cathedral, the sweeping-away-of-trifles which was his spirit, has banished the organ from the nave and built it up again over the colossal west door. The rearrangement of the interior has necessitated the disturbance of old graves in the floor. When the workmen reach evidence of ancient burial a canon in his surplice stands above the violated grave and directs the removal of the remains. A singular scene it is from the gloom of the door. The solemnity of Herrera's lofty and unbending spirit fills the remodelled temple. Even the light from the concealed lunettes of the clerestory falls in a wide and even flood. Workmen bend and grope, and to the gestures of the robed priest the skulls of those long dead are piled in baskets while the sunlight travels slowly along the aisle illuminating one by one the iron lilies, upright above the rows of penitential boxes lining the wall.

To one soldier his iron lily, to another his adventure. While Herrera piled stone in Valladolid, Cervantes with his one hand and his limp built a temple for laughter and set it up in Europe. The shabby house in a back street was no more shabby than great men have often lived in. (Who knows to this day where Columbus died in this same old capital city of Spain?) It was 'a little place for so much grandeur', as Charles V said of the funeral vault at Granada, but grandeur will leak and spill, and the police incident which drew unwanted attention to the apartment of Don Miguel de Cervantes during his lifetime at least served to label a shrine for Spain and a heritage for the world.

SOMETHING SEEN

A woman sits all day in the shelter of the arcade selling fruit. She sits on a low stool against a pillar. Two flat baskets are on a trestle beside her. In the winter she has oranges shining in vivid piles under the archway; then cherries; then apricots and peaches. She is always in the black dress and severe little shawl worn by the decent women of the people. Though she is middle-aged she sits upright as the pillar against which she places her baskets. A pleasing figure to look at and of great dignity, she has always a large book open upon her knee from which she reads in the intervals of business. We pass this woman reading her book in the shadow day after day. She never seems to finish it. 'Do you know what it can be?' we ask a Spanish friend! 'Oh! if it is an old book and a large book and she never comes to an end, it will be a religious book', he decides; 'but at any rate let us ask her!'

The fruit-seller coloured a little at the question, not with offence but modesty.

'Might she lend it to us if we were interested? It lacked the first few pages but we might take it willingly if we cared to."

We turned over the pages. The title was missing, but at the head of every page, yellow, decorated with stiff little woodcuts, we found the theme of her book.

'Los lloros de los Pobres.' (The sorrows of the poor.) That is what she reads all day and every day, seated in the town arcade beside her piles of fruit.

'It is a very old story,' she says apologetically as we return her book to her: 'Una novela antigua!'

Chapter Nine

SEGOVIA

'EL PUENTE'

'That's the aqueduct, Señora! *made here!*' piped a small boy, skilfully avoiding retribution by pretending he wasn't there.

It sounded funny, yet it was perfectly true. There is certainly something alien and dark and formidable about this enormous muscular stretch of the empire of Augustus across the bright Spanish town of Segovia, yet it was in every particular 'made there', part of a piece of practical Roman building and town-planning, built with granite from local hills, with the minimum weight of material for its two-tiered arches, its inscription a bold label of copper letters, the whole as serviceable and local as a railway viaduct. Size and endurance are impressive always, but one looks across the Roman Campagna at the aqueducts of the Caesars broken amid cornfields and grazing-lands, with other reflections than those which visit one at the sight of this grey arm which reaches water to the town, serving (until last year) its original intention as it did before the birth of Christ, reaching through legend and empire, becoming a feature and responsibility of the town's life, acquiring even in the end a familiar name among the people, becoming indeed, 'El Puente'.

Something of anxiety attaches to its maintenance in hard frost by those responsible for the town's monuments. Something of courage, too, for the rise and recovery of so many small Spanish cities is often dwarfed by the impressive ruins of their history. No building so Herculean could have survived the Middle Ages without acquiring the legend of dark origins. The Devil built it to please a Spanish princess, and by black arts stayed the going down of the sun until its completion. The aqueduct profoundly impressed Isabella, herself a conscious builder of empire and not immediately concerned with the expulsion of any Romans. Her good sense dictated that it should be restored exactly as it had been built, and though the difference in the later building is apparent, it is not derogatory. The work was carried through by a friar of El Parral, and since he is reputed to have had no reward other than the honour, let him have at least that in the perpetuation of his name, Fray Juan Escovedo.

How strange it is that the placing of one stone on another should have produced this mighty bridge bestriding the small city of Segovia with its curiously economical slender arches, which, packed close in profile, are like the heavily buttressed façade of some enormous palace—the hugest 'dry-stone dyke' ever built. From the opposite side of the valley El Puente seems more akin to the hills than to the town. When other buildings are absorbed in sunlight, becoming slender and fragile in bulk, this dark granite bridge becomes even darker and more solid in appearance, like the iron rocks in the Sierras, lighting as the mountains light and saddening to their tone.

The traffic and clatter of the market, the fashions and gossip, the worldliness and piety of Segovian centuries have passed underneath it, for the city built on a rock stands upon layer on layer of history, its modern prosperity and self-respect basking agreeably in a wonderful natural situation beneath the haven of the Guadarramas. It seems indeed to partake more of the nature of the mountains with their variety than of the plain of Castile with its simplicities and austerities. Riding high like other cities of Castile—Cuenca, Toledo, Arévalo—its prow for ever dividing two floods which meet and clamour beneath the sharp rocks of its keel, one is to imagine how the entire silhouette and mass of the town on the hill was changed by the building of the late-Gothic cathedral; how the fortified houses with their towers became interesting and detached survivals, yielding their place of dominance to the planning of the architect Gil de Hontañón.[1] They are stately, these ancient towers, and beautiful still, bearing the outside plaster decoration which would seem one of the few Moorish traces in this town, this style of plaster-cutting and stamping, repeated in modern houses and later buildings, notably the Alcázar, becoming a not un-

[1] Gil de Hontañón. The two architects, Juan Gil the father and Rodrigo Gil the son, were responsible for the building of both Seville and Segovia Cathedrals—the son taking up the father's plans and work, 1522–1577.

successful mode of decoration, peculiar, it would seem, to Segovia.

El Puente is not the only unusually complete 'stone of remembrance' in Segovian history. The church of La Vera Cruz, deposited by the short and powerful reign of the Templars, is, in its way, as curious and arresting, with its lighting, and its central double chapel, in the upper chamber of which the knight kept vigil before the armour laid on its rough stone altar on the night of his consecration. One pays respect also to the house of Alvaro de Luna, Constable of Castile, though it wears no hidalgo's cloak any longer, but only the tattered black *capa* of the *carbonero* (charcoal-burner). One peeps into the patio with curiosity, remembering the house of his kinsman and foe in the old Asturian capital, Santillana. The hood-moulding of granite over its entrance is repeated with dignified effect in other patrician houses of the town. Fortunately for those who wander about the streets of Segovia the greatest beauty of its innumerable churches is their exterior. So many have been reconstructed within that they are past recovery. But the number of beautiful Romanesque façades, doors, and arcaded galleries showing to the street, even in buildings no longer holding the cult, is a delightful architectural possession. The outside galleries have a delicate architectural effect, giving a sense of space to spare in a narrow street, like the patio in the close ways of Córdoba, and enriching the severity of the early façades with the grace of their slender colonnades. The Romanesque tower of San Esteban which in Street's[1] day was lamentably out of repair, so that it became the fashion to suppose it would never be restored, stands now complete,

[1] G. E. Street, author of *Gothic Architecture in Spain*, the authoritative book in English on that style of building in Spain.

the lovely tower with its angle columns adding to its originality and grace, seemly and compact, its roof simplified and suitable. When restoration is done as well as this it becomes fine architecture.

From beneath all the history of its monuments modern Segovia wakes up at Eastertime to the customs of summer. The mantilla appears again in place of the winter cloak, the officers wear summer uniform. The chairs of the cafés are put on the pavement, and the *paseo* increases in animation. Newspapers are full of the processions at Seville and the number of tourists who have thronged to the town. *Blanco y Negro*, *La Estampa*, *La Esfera* publish the histories of the famous crucifixes and images carried in procession. In the nave of the cathedral (so unusually bright for a Spanish church) one is impressed by the uniform blackness of a Spanish congregation. There is a great assembly of poor people: women and girls with black veils over their hair, standing, sitting on the floor, kneeling. The men crowd to the big pillars of the aisles. There is a high platform with benches before the bronze gates dividing sanctuary from choir. People wait with that patience in their attitude which always reminds the Northerner of the Oriental. Children push in the crowd and are lifted to see better. Gleams of light are thrust from an opening and closing door. Soon it lies in a steady wave on the faces of the congregation, turned to watch the entry of the bishop. Two rows of old men wearing white shirts and black *capas* seat themselves on the benches upon the platform. Rigid and severe in outline, grey heads, white front, long black *capa*, they sit motionless. Now the space between the two black lines is filled with all possible ecclesiastical gold and purple, of the bishop and his attendant canons. The contrast is pictorial and significant.

The Aqueduct, Segovia

Apse of San Tirzo, Sahagún

Kneeling boys hold open the missal from which the bishop reads the office. The choir intone a chant. One by one the bishop lays aside his silver staff, his ring, his jewelled cross, his vestments. In the white tunic of a monk he 'girds himself with a towel' and in a silver basin washes and dries the feet of the twelve poor men of the town. Having done this he resumes his garments and seats himself on his throne while a Carmelite friar paints the lesson of the scene with all Castilian eloquence.

All the day of Good Friday there has been a small table standing at the gate of the prison, upon it a crucifix veiled in purple and a large pewter salver. Two soldiers of the Civil Guard sit within the shadow of the outer court of the prison. By night the salver is full of coins, for the prisoners' Easter festival. For the evening of the processions of the *pasos* the prisoners are in a room looking on to the street. It is after dark when the *pasos* reach the prison, light from the candles making a faint moonlight in the street. The lights glimmer upon the prison façade, and from within barred windows hands are stretched out to the enthroned figures, and *saetas* fly through the bars in piercing appeal. The procession lingers as long as it may. The little boys of the seminary, holding their candles crooked, look up with scared innocent faces. For this one night the prisoners are as other men, joining in their festival. What wonder that this escape of voice and soul is tasted to the full. Each *paso* is delayed by the *saetas* to the last limit of the possible. Then lights and figures leave the façade blind again and silent with a more tragic and lonely silence.

When a town claims an artist as its man of eminence, it should be put on record how it came about. Daniel Zuloaga, of Basque family though born in Madrid, came to Segovia for a visit and fell in love with 'El ambiente de Segovia'. Having seen San Juan de los Caballeros in the dignity of its ruin, he became 'mad' for love of it and finally bought it. Its restoration he accomplished with great artistic care, and within it established his family and the work of ceramics for which he left his earlier work as a painter, though never, I believe, completely.

Segovia is not, like Avila, in the grand manner, but its amenities are unusually gracious. In the springtime, when the hoopoe's soft threefold call and strange barred wing visit the orchards, and the force of mountain waters comes to the town, borne on the endurance of the Roman channel, how El Puente frames the background of the hill city ('el ambiente' which Daniel Zuloaga 'went mad for'), those blue steeps and lilac snows of the Guadarramas; how, in the glitter and joy and penetration of the sunlight the blossoming trees wind about the hill like some fair Easter procession, and the undulating Downlands, vivid with springing corn, begin their journey to harvest from the base of twofold snows!

Chapter Ten

AVILA

IN THE GRAND MANNER

Eighty-six towers and nine gates of glowing bronze! What vivid blazonry of history was this which the July evening sun made of the walls of Avila? For an hour this untouchable and terrible city flamed against the sky. Then the sun sank and the patient granite walls were pale again in the lowering evening. Avila became once more the turreted imagination of antique parchment missals, more medieval than her history and less real; the heraldic emblem, the citadel of Castile and of ancient Catholic Spain. From the distant plain, shining in the delicate upland summer, the fortifications of Avila gleam, as visionary as the retreating towers of romance. Then they become unapproachable cliffs with golden seas flooding to their base. Close beneath, the unpeopled towers guard a searching silence, their sentries the storks motionless on the gates and belfries, their men-at-arms the swallows, their flying arrows the blue darts of myriad and living wings. From the cross on the opposite hill the mass of her climbing towers is so formidable that it is hard to believe any town ever needed such defence. They remain now symbol and monument of the great dead of Avila. High on their turrets the storks stand in delicate silhouette against the sky, immovable, like the devices on a coat of arms. Every year, and always on the day of San Blas,[1] one or two appear on the towers, to fly when the harvest is reaped, like the fireflies in Tuscany, watchmen, it would seem, of the green and growing corn.

The shrewdness of the winter in this town lying solitary in a wide plain as high as the top of Ben Nevis is one of the first facts remembered of Avila. Its second is Santa Teresa. Yet in the sweet summer evening which illuminates the city like a late love, I was shown Santa Teresa's guitar, her tabor too, and her reed-pipes.

It is not easy to capture the summer enchantment of these austere uplands. The purity of the air in these altitudes, and the infinite soft horizons of gold, the harvest kindling in the high sun of July, instead of the hanging September light of England; the simplicity and spareness of the landscape; the outline of elusive Sierras broken with hints of snow; the quick emerald banners of the trees, marching beside the golden harvest like decisions—the decisions an artist makes for good or ill in his pictures—set the towers of Avila on a rich and glowing shield. On a field Or and Vert, a city with towers, Argent! So much is Avila in the grand manner, that even her prosperity is maintained from nothing less august

[1] San Blas. Saint Blaise, patron of wool-combers.

than the ancient dignities of sowing and harvest; explained by the corn fields, mellow and full of savour in the strong highland air. The sweet bread of Avila is succulent and sound as no other in Spain. The threshing-floors spread like encamping armies over the plain, refining the flaming and living gold to the pallor of grain; antique and classic as the vintage of Sulmona, and with a Roman origin.

It was Avila which once set the standard measure for the grain-growers of Castile. The little local book (Señor Fernández) on the antiquities of Avila is full of detail gathered from old chronicles of the regulations for fairs and markets, for the control of inn-keepers and the scrutiny of the guests they entertained, for the standardizing of measures of grain, and how the measure used by Avila was the standard adopted by Mexico.

'Blasphemy and begging are prohibited in this capital' says the notice placed on each gate of the city, and Avila deals dutifully with its poor outside the gate of San Vicente. To one side of a plaza planted with trees which bears the impress of an old market-place is a long stone building. 'Comedor de Caridad.' Granite blocks make seats in the shade, and, like a darker shadow underneath, old women sit there motionless, the black dress of Spanish decency hiding all except their faces. Twice a day to this plaza converges the broken procession. The old women of the town come early, since poverty and old age are rich in leisure. But as the meal-hour approaches figures rise from beneath trees, and men hasten on the road as they catch sight of the gate and its promise. Pigs and dogs come too, and lie down beside the worldly possessions of the unfortunate. Men drop bundles and lean on the long peeled staff of the road, all walkers in this country of riders. There is a foreground of Goya still beneath the gate of San Vicente outside the walls of Avila.

As we entered Avila (Avila de los Caballeros) the town was stirred by the funeral of the *grand seigneur* the Duque de Parcent. What throngs there were of poor people in the streets, and cripples lying about the gate of the church, thrusting, begging, chattering! Inside the obscure nave two rows of tall candles outlined the last state of the Duke. Voices chanted above the silence of the mourners. August people were in the funeral procession, but behind the red cord what pushing and chattering and press of poverty! 'Afterwards alms were distributed to the poor from the gate of the palace.' It was like the funeral of the Master of Ravenswood. (To-day the Madrid paper announces that there is to be a census taken of all the beggars in Spain.)

The practical working of this feudal system is an 'affair of Spain', but architecturally a Spanish city is always made imposing and interesting by the inclusion of seignorial houses. The palacio adds dignity and 'presence' to the streets, the carving of its great portal an air to the plaza, and there are palaces of fine architectural importance within the walls of Avila. The cathedral crowns the summit, being itself part of the fortification, its magnificent apse forming one of the towers of the wall, from a distance looking like a miniature Castel Sant' Angelo, couching high and quiet, a dragon with a sting in its tail.

The aristocratic town house in which Santa Teresa was born has been made into a dreary church. But one looks from within the town gate across the wide plain made for adventures, unchanged still, across which the high-spirited little girl, whose mother read books of chivalry and whose father studied the Lives of the Saints, set off for martyrdom. Rapture, logic, instant decision and action—these characteristics never changed in Teresa. Heaven was for ever and ever and ever! All the saints said so! Then why waste *any* time on earth? Why not go to heaven at once, and, being of a great house, why not in the grand manner? Ah! that heaven of the saints! She was to reach it, but not by martyrdom. That vigorous integrity, that generous large nature, that courage were needed for work, and for the endurance of heat and labour.

It is a pity that no other contemporary portrait was left of the great saint of Avila than a dull monkish painting. 'God forgive you, Brother! After putting me to all that trouble you have made me very old and very ugly!' was her own cheerful outspoken comment on the tedious and uninstructed work of the painter.

Language must always be of its own period, and the ardours of Saint Teresa were expressed in that of her day. Though her triumph and renown fill all Spain and Europe, to-day only eighteen nuns in the convent of the Encarnación follow her rule, and but twenty-one in San José. But her title of honour throughout all Spain is Doctora Mística, and her full-blooded flexible Castilian writing her abiding monument. In the Encarnación outside Avila one is shown the block of wood which was her pillow, her guitar, and harp. In San José a faint old voice speaks for a while from behind a turntable, remote as from a distant life. Then the turntable lumbers round, and one by one the woman in the sacristy lays on the table the relics of the saint—the book which determined her religious life, her 'flute' (two reed-pipes which accompany the tabor), and her tabor with silver bells.

'When did she play them?'

'On Nochebuena when the Child was born, she used to play to the nuns in the convent.' Joy was among the saintly attributes, and one likes to think of Teresa of Jesus, shaken as she was by the deep tempest of a noble intolerance, fighting as few ever fought for her own integrity of soul, her spiritual history among the noble classics of a noble language, playing so gay and merry a music to her nuns in the cloister.

I am called in question when I say that Avila is the most Spanish city in Spain, yet I persist, for here more than anywhere one feels the heart of a race at once virile and courtly, vigorous and independent. Avila's independence was the last to yield to Charles V. Her records are full of the names and deeds of hidalgos, and the grand manner is Avila's lawful inheritance in history. Do the walls of Avila cramp as well as defend?

'Look at it, Señora!' said a voice at my side. 'Isn't it ugly? Nothing but those hard strong walls! Have you seen Seville?'

THE BELL-RINGER'S CHILDREN

'The cathedral tower commands a fine view' says the guide-book. From beneath in the plaza, one has watched the birds circling, the bells hung in their canopy, the clock, the brick loggia squeezed among the battlements. Then one idle day the desire comes to see what the birds see, to possess their horizon.

The cripple boy who has the key of the tower door is delighted. He rings a bell at its base, and a woman's voice calls from high within the tower. One can see her head leaning over to watch who is coming up. In the gallery at the end of the first stair the guide is waiting, a serious little girl with a lantern almost as big as herself, for the second part of the stair is perfectly dark.

What a magnificent chamber the bells and the clock

inhabit, immense, vaulted, silent! The little girl is especially proud of the works of the clock, that mysterious mechanism which directs all the affairs of the town below. She can hardly be got to leave the great room which seems to her much better worth visiting than the view of all the summer corn fields and sierras.

'Do the storks build on the tower?' we ask as we climb the stair.

'Oh! the storks! How dirty they are! Sticks flying everywhere, getting into everything. We threw their nests down until they went and built in another place. What dirty things!'

Two tiny children trot across the roof to join us; each one is perhaps as high as one of the steep steps of the stairway. Something in the nature of a treat is about to happen. So much one gathers. The elder sister grasps her lantern. The two babies, with delighted crab-like sidlings, accomplish the first part of the journey.

'Now the night begins!' solemnly chants the child with the lantern. Giggles of joy announce that the treat has arrived. To climb up and down this funnel of adventure and dark with a lantern, to have for nursery the great clock chamber, to man the battlements against the storks, to look on the street below from the height of the bells! What a world the bell-ringer's children enjoy all alone in the tower of the cathedral!

Narrow passages where the darkness is like a cold vapour lead to their playground on the cathedral fortifications. Up to these the lame boy hoists himself too, for he also lives at the top of the tower. The babies gather wild flowers from the ramparts soft with grass. Tufts of valerian and spurges grow in the wall. From between the battlements they can see the street below. 'Hola, Paco!' 'Hola, Ignacio!' they shout to acquaintances, waiting with delight for the surprised glance around.

'You have the highest house in the town!'

'*And* the most beautiful!' says the lame boy.

'*And* the coldest', says the mother.

'There is *one* stork's nest here!' The lame boy points to a ledge out-of-reach below. 'Two eggs in it!' join in the others. They disappear into the dark again. In a few moments excited faces peer upwards from the battlements. The children emerge in a mass.

'*Bats!*' announces the lame boy. 'It is the best time to catch them when they are asleep!' They have strings of the clinging uncanny haul. Difficult to tell whether they are dead or alive, but throw them wide into the air from the battlements and they will decide for themselves. If they are alive they wake up and fly, if they are dead they drop. Now is the solemn moment. There are ceremonies in the tower unknown to the priests below. The requiem for dead bats is an office unknown to the canon, but it makes a fine reverberation up in the tower above the roofs. As each bat drops the children chant aloud, as a precaution in case it might be dead, 'Lux perpetua, Domine!' 'Requiem aeternam, Domine!' The air is soon full of whirling awakened bats. 'Bats are good to eat!' says the lame boy, but he finds them better playthings in this tower above the swallows. There is no end to the working of a great cathedral it seems!

IN THE ALAMEDA

It is the festival of Corpus. Since Easter everything has been directed to this greatest of Catholic celebrations. Plays, *verbenas*, fireworks, and dances are to take place. The town is preparing illuminations. In the Alameda a convent school is pacing slowly, a group of cheerful nuns in attendance on the children. They are watching the preparations. It is so much a holiday that the nuns have brought luncheon for their pupils. They are to sit in the fragrant shade out of doors and eat it, a holiday for the nuns as well as the children, innocent and animated. Now the children may scatter and play in the Alameda for an hour. The sisters seat themselves happily on the grass, free also. The Alameda crowns a ridge of ground. On the farther side of the little wood the ground dips down to a goat-track leading to the hills. Ah, Satan! Three gipsy girls, swaying, light of foot, nimble of eye, wheedling of tongue, are coming up that path; carnations in their hair, 'the world' in the frills of their bright pink skirts and sky-blue mantones. On one side of the ridge sit the sisters tranquil and happy. On the other is a row of little faces excited and inquisitive, and gipsy girls smoothing soft childish palms. Tittering and half-frightened exclamations hover about the group like the twittering of birds. The whistle blows. The children scamper at the sound. 'Handsome husband! Fine house! Winner in the lottery!' Ah! convent dormitories, what dreams will you shelter to-night!

Chapter Eleven

LEÓN

PULCHRA LEONINA

Where the Cathedral of León rides high and gallant and beautiful, like some noble ship buoyed and flying under full sail, there is visible also from the plain the old Gate of Castile and the two circular bays of the ancient fort which is now the prison; type of that old León which under pressure of modern prosperity is being abandoned, becoming 'French and fine', or left to the outskirts of the town until such time as it can be remembered. So rapidly is the town being rebuilt and its old two-storied houses with their arcades disappearing, that even within two visits of a year old landmarks are gone, streets are paved, and new gardens planted round the cathedral with seats of ceramics from Segovia recording the shabby pictorial León of which the prison and the walls about it will keep the longest record.

Daring and beautiful, 'Pulchra Leonina' rises above the small town of León, as Ely above its meadows, discerned from afar in that plain with horizons like a sea, on whose distances a mountain and a town are discovered high and alone, like remote unvisited lands. Looking out from the city across the wide desert of its river-bed, the hills stand blue and sunny as the hills of Morven, in the shrewd October air, and the river (linked pools of azure in the grey plain of stones) sends a vibration of rippling colour beneath miles of golden poplars. The tawny and lazy León of August, with the sun pressing hard on the wayfarer across the plain, the hills gashed and incised as though some giant etcher had chosen to empty all his waste corrosives over them, is quickened in the windy light, and green and happy places signalled by forests of poplars.

Between its soldier and its saint the Leonese citizens take the air in the modern Alameda by the river, and the new street reaches to the cathedral. For old tumble-down León one looks in the plazas and outskirts, to the church of 'Our Lady of the Market', to the fountains of Charles IV, to the convent of the Concepción with its Spanish savour, part grandiose, part ascetic, part melancholy, closed with the Oriental wooden lattice, to the few remaining aristocratic houses fallen into squalor, and on the peasants coming in on their donkeys, wrapped in plaids and seated on sheep-skins, quite unaware that the world is changing before their eyes.

'Sutileza' is the quality claimed by the Leonese for their beautiful church. 'Daring', one might also say, looking at the slenderness of the piers which support this high-bred and delicate beauty of Gothic art. The portals, unusually low on the west façade, give one easy access to their sculpture (the coarser work on the pillars standing to show how something better was once arranged) and one is able to reflect upon the change in manner from the early Romanesque sculpture to that of the newer Gothic. Something benign and serious and simple which one associates with Romanesque has given way to elegance and grace. The garden of Paradise with its musicians might be (perhaps *was*) the garden of a queen's court, and stepping from the region of the placid remote Madonna, 'Nuestra Señora la Blanca' becomes alive and astir with grace and charm.

'There's no doubt', said my architect friend, 'that stained glass is the greater part of Gothic.' So that one must make up one's mind early about the graceful house of glass which the unknown architect built up here in the serious sunlight of Spain. If Street was amazed at the bravery of the four-light triforium windows with the clerestory blocked in, what would he have said to the six-light triforium of to-day and a clerestory now answering its original purpose of letting in the sunlight! From the necessity the architect was under, of building upon the town wall, the lights are placed very high so that their glories shine far above the eye's ordinary journey. The colours, save for some weary modern strips, are of magnificent fullness. The light, entangled there as among the clouds of sunset, comes suavely to the interior, and the buoyancy and grace of the sanctuary thus glorified brings real delight, as at the successfully vibrating high note of a song. I would go a long way to surprise, too, the black robe of San Antonio de Padua in his blue window holding a child like a precious jewel, and the amber and gold of San Clemente as they stand together at the end of the side aisle, a whole eyeful of pleasure illuminating the dusk.

One wants, apparently, in thrusting against the sky such a light and delicate design, to have and hold captive all the colours of all the sunsets in the world in heavenly suggestion; the jewellery of Paradise cut in sunbeams; the hint of splendours beyond mortal, which this lovely art designed to live in the light alone can give. Being sure of the excellence of your glass you will dare much, and never has daring been so near the disaster of courage as this high flight of Gothic in León. The narrowness of the cathedral helps, no doubt, the acrobatic span of the flying buttresses; one holds one's breath at the feat, as at the balance of a tight-rope walker, but it is *done* and

'Sint licet Hispanis ditissima pulchraque templa,
Hoc tamen egregiis omnibus arte prius.'[1]

is no arrogant claim.

The Spanish genius adopted for its own a sumptuous Romanesque, and the Romanesque gives little opportunity for the magical wandering of light through painted transparencies. So that if Burgos, León, and Toledo had never been attempted, Spain would have lacked its full measure of this fragile and lovely art.

Throughout the cathedral, delicacy and a certain aristocratic grace of gait seem to have passed. The tomb of Ordoño II[2] is that of a kingly person, had he no Gothic and golden crown. There is more painting of a fine exalted nature than in most Spanish churches—carving, where it

[1] 'Sint licet Hispanis', etc. Quoted both by Street and Ford as having been inscribed on a stone above the main porch of the cathedral, near Nuestra Señora la Blanca. The inscription is no longer there.

[2] Ordoño II, 913–923. Visigothic king who held a great court at León. He presented his palace for the early basilica on the site of which the cathedral now stands.

occurs on the elegant piers, is fine filigree; where sculpture is storied, as in the tombs, it is grave and beautiful.

In the chapel of 'Our Lady of the High-road' behind the tomb of Ordoño II a faint light was shining and a slow droning hymn, very respectful and low-toned, sounded in the ambulatory. Two candles burned before the *reja* in sockets on the floor, and within the chapel a peasant was kneeling before the altar steps. On the altar Our Lady of the Road supported the fallen body of her Son across her knees. Seriously, slowly, line by line as he remembered the words, the peasant sang his hymn. Beside him was a large clean bundle and his staff. Everything he knew of music and respect went into his hymn. When it was finished he rose, sealed his forehead, eyes, and lips with the sign of the cross, and passed out to his journey. The peasant of the reign of Ordoño II would have done no other.

The soldier and the churchman so often merge in Spanish history, with its early fortified churches, its religious military orders, and its wars of intolerance, that one takes for granted a soldier and a bishop in any town of ancient history. Yet Guzmán the Good and San Isidoro, who typify the spirit of León, were both active in life in the south of Spain—San Isidoro being the erudite Archbishop of Seville, and Guzmán the Governor of Tarifa in the second Moorish invasion. The Roman deed of the soldier upon the wall of Tarifa, which rings like the clang of his dagger on the pavement, is here commemorated at the entrance to the town.

Alonzo Guzmán, having undertaken the defence of Tarifa, which had been won by Sancho the Brave from the Moors, had lent his boy of nine as a page to the Infante Don Juan, brother to Sancho. The brother, turning traitor, treasonably led the Moors to the siege of the town and calling for the

Governor offered these terms. The boy, his son, whom he led before the eyes of the father beneath the wall, would be spared if the father surrendered the town. If he refused, the child would be there and then put to death. The answer of the loyalist father was to draw his own dagger and throw it to the traitor for the consummation of the infamy.

The body of San Isidoro (more honourably lodged than his Master's) is in a silver coffin above the altar of the church which bears his name, one of the noblest Romanesque buildings in Spain. From San Isidoro's histories came knowledge of the early peoples of Iberia, and accounts of great buildings and law-giving. The Suevi, Vandals, and Goths owe the preservation of their history to Saint Isidore in Spain, and his arrangement of the earlier liturgies of the Spanish Church were those finally accepted for use throughout the country. In the church of San Isidoro is incorporated also the Pantheon of the Kings, where, since the chapel of St. Gabriel with its painted ceiling and walls was uncovered in Canterbury Cathedral, the English visitor may compare with it the noble painting of the same date which decorates the ceiling of this royal sepulchral chamber, all in astonishing preservation.

The book of words of Leonese history is housed in the old Plateresque (see p. 129) convent of San Marcos, from Roman altars and the tombs of the Seventh Legion who kept León from forays in the north to the lovely Gothic and Romanesque figures from Corullón and Sahagún.

Gaudí the modern has not been left out of the architecture of progressive León, and in the midst of the wide agricultural plain around it, the new generation constructs its ideals. There is a model farm just outside the town, 'A Grange', charmingly planned, and with pedigree stock. The entrance, with its hygienic buildings, is planted with a flower-garden, and on one side the attention is attracted to model hen-houses of olive and white ceramics bearing these four inscriptions over the doors:

'*The flowers and fruits of this Grange belong to the town and are cultivated for the refreshment and use of the town. In respecting the rights of all, each therefore respects his own.*'

'*Ask the blessing of God upon your fields and herds, but do not let idleness and apathy make profitless the care and labour of Providence.*'

'*The animals and plants are the most splendid manifestation of Nature's vigour. To make selection of species is to be lord of the forces of Nature.*'

'*If every visitor to this Grange experiences a stirring of the spirit at the sight of this expanding life here made visible before him, the provincial deputation will consider their work fruitful and exalted.*'

The incurable Don Quixote in the Spaniard!

The Kingdom of León is mostly typified for me by an air both shrewd and scorching, by long roads on undulating lands never out of sight of hills, by pueblos which one enters and passes out of, whose yellow earthen houses keep an Eastern secrecy, but most by its wide river-bed across which, some twenty miles from the town of León, we scrambled to find the church of San Miguel de Escalada.

The rippling of poplars on distant banks of stone showed how far the river's breadth extended, but only the blue shallows of summer animated the vast plain of pebbles. Strings of mules burdened like an Eastern caravan defiled to the brim of the water. Oxen stood immobile, yoked to their primitive chariots on the stones of the river-bed, as if at the burial of Alaric, King of the Visigoths, in the bed of the river

Busento. Sheep followed their shepherd as over the desert. It is a sign of mid-summer in Spain when the men go to work at the safety of the rivers. Here, pent in the dam which twenty or thirty men were building, was the captive and essential current, a formidable volume of water enough to those who balanced on the dam at its edge. This crossed, with the plain of pebbles, a swampy ground beyond, with lively streams, led over planks and logs to a steep gully. A scramble upwards on the slope of a sandy hill and we were in the retreat of the monks who fled from Córdoba in the year 913 to be lost as far as might be in the middle of León.

It was like finding a hostel in a desert. The hard, scorched earth rose around it. Desolate thistles and grasses rustled about its portico. No one will disturb the archaeologist save the wind as he spells the confused but legible history of this Christian refuge. It is harder to dislodge a place of worship than an army, it seems. Bricks unearthed in the excavations of the floor bear the stamp of the seventh Roman legion who occupied León. Visigothic inscriptions have been found in the capitals (Lampérez). So that probable dates reach far back to an earlier building given to and restored by the Córdoban monks. But the church granted to the monks was made ready by them for consecration in the year 914 by the bishop who took up the work and place of San Fructuoso in the Bierzo, San Genadio, Bishop of Astorga. Certain similarities of building in another church consecrated by this bishop in the year 919, San Pedro de Montes, and yet another founded by Córdoban monks in 921, have suggested that one Mozárabe architect designed all three. His name Viviano is known from an inscription in San Pedro de Montes, and Professor Gómez Moreno advances the theory that the Bishop Genadio, impressed by the building of San Miguel, brought the architect to the building of San Pedro in the mountains, and later to the church in Sanabria.

A 'Mozárabe church of the Latin type', saved by its isolation and abandoned for its poverty, it stands across the safety of its wide flood. It was one of the features of the Mozárabe churches that the walls were undecorated. The slender and graceful colonnades bearing their horseshoe arches give the style of a venerable temple to this hidden place. Where did all those elegant pagan columns come from in the forsaken districts of Spain? They are of marble, and those of the Eikonostasis support a deep moulding carved in geometrical patterns like the Visigothic remains in Mérida. The decorated stone slabs which separate presbytery from church have been put in position again by those in charge of national monuments, and the primitive stone tables which served as altars set in their places. So that the effect is not abandoned nor tragic as of pious things fallen out of mind. The quiet atmosphere of the student has enveloped San Miguel, and the wide spaces of Spain are its background. The setting sun searched it out on its eminence as we slipped and scrambled over the vast river plain. Then the Kingdom of León absorbed it, and we saw it no more.

Chapter Twelve

VILLAFRANCA DEL BIERZO

EL BIERZO

The murmuring of trees and streams as clear over their brown pebbles as the waters of Tweed, the shadow of silent mountains against the grave blue night, for a time the music of a guitar, then only the undertone of the three valley rivers and a musical chant lifted every hour,

> *La—a Una—a! Y—y Sereno—o!*
> *Las — Dos! Y—y Nublado—o!*

and one turns to sleep content in the country town of Villafranca del Bierzo, where the medieval pilgrims halted under the protection of the Templars of Ponferrada on their way to Santiago de Compostela.

'There are no Serenos in England? Then who watches the town when it sleeps?' inquired our friends of the Círculo.

'But you can see', explained the advocate, 'how the Sereno is a great convenience to a small town. For instance, if any one falls ill in the night you open your window, strike palms together for the Sereno and ask him to do you the favour of fetching a doctor. A gratification, of course, for his services, but one can see that it is a great convenience. This town supports three.' That call in the night sounds up the valley with a strange sense of reassurance and safety. I am not sure that the country night without it wouldn't now lack some invisible comfort.

The happy valley of El Bierzo, over which San Fructuoso, the 'prince of the royal blood of the Visigoths', ruled until he fled from his dignity to a hermit's sanctuary, and into whose seclusions he penetrated deeper and deeper for solitude from the inconveniences of sanctity, is, in summer-time, one of the most coloured and fruitful beauties of Spain. These sweetnesses of landscape are not many in this land where nature is splendid and royal, and it is not surprising that those who entered the valley for the fame of the hermit-prince should have chosen to stay, until forty monasteries came to be built there with sanctuaries and chapels without number.

Looking across the valley in the level evening sunlight, great scars of aureolin upon the gravity of the mountain purple show the gold mines for which the Asturians and later the Romans penetrated the Cantabrian mountains. In this 'Siberia of Roman captives' the mines were worked for three centuries, for a tribute of 20,000 pounds of gold was required from the three provinces of Galicia, Lusitania, and Asturias. 'From no country in the world was finer gold taken than from Spain. Not only did they take minerals from the mountains, but the rivers ran gold.' To-day, beneath *las Médulas* (still showing clearly the engineering canals and cisterns and shafts of the Romans) the washerwomen wash the sand of the river for occasional grains of gold which can be sold for a few pesetas.

One sets sail, as it were, in the sunny valley to find the remains of the early sanctuaries and monasteries which followed the flight of San Fructuoso from his own holiness. The history of many is now the history of Santa Marina, which Ford notes as a very old church one league towards Corullón.

'Santa Marina? I can show you where it was, but it has disappeared. One or two old people remember it, but it was very ancient, and the river and the earth and the chestnut trees little by little overcame it. There was a big monastery of friars attached to it and for a long time people used to dredge the banks of the river for the monks' treasure, and not long ago they came on the foundations of the church deep in the earth, silted up by the rains and river. And then, one day, a man gathering chestnuts in an old tree put out his hand to reach a branch and sounded a bell which had been surrounded by growing branches and remained in the tree. So that one knows exactly where it was, but little by little it was covered by the chestnut trees and the silting of earth, and now there is no church at all, only the name.'

So one finds the memories growing fainter; only names left, or now and then a fragment in a museum, delicate marble figures from Carracedo; *estufado* [1] figures of great grace and beauty from San Esteban of Corullón within a

[1] *Estufado* figures seem to have been evolved from a rag doll or a mummy. They are made apparently of layers of linen cloths, treated by some process to make the mass plastic, and then modelled with charming results. The linen material is heavily painted and varnished on the outside, giving rather the effect of a painted wooden figure of delicate modelling.

stone's throw of Santa Marina. How closely one cult followed another, for within the same wood is another Romanesque church of San Juan Bautista, and San Miguel stands close to both, lofty and beautiful among the chestnuts.

In the town of Villafranca, close under the mountains, shady with chestnut woods, rippling with vines and rivers, medieval history moulders away with its architecture. From the castle a long street of patrician houses marches the entire length of the town with eaves as wide as those of a Florentine palace. The one fortified house left in the town, with deep exterior galleries and stabling quarters for men-at-arms, now gives its cool obscurity to the enormous wine-casks which store the harvests of the warm hill-slopes. Surprises await one in these wine vaults, full of vats as large as elephants, of shadows and must. In the gloom of the heavy old fortified house a voice fell among us from some obscurity near the roof. There was a scuffling, and the bulky figure of an old Spanish gentleman descended the ladder from the top of a wine-cask. On the ground he embraced the Scotsman among us with eloquent effusions as something longed for but seldom met.

'As a boy, and from early youth', he explained, 'ever since I read about her I have cherished a devotion for the Reina María of Scotland. For *her* sake all Scotsmen are dear to me. It is a *great*, a profound devotion I have cherished for the Reina María. Her countrymen are to me as my own relations.'

'He is', our companion explained with obvious distaste in the street outside, 'very religious, a bigot.'

On the other side of the long street the Inquisition held state, and Torquemada's palace, a noble Renaissance building, 'battered and decayed' and now the day-school, is of central importance (the Spaniards will point out the aptness of the coat of arms with its canting device, 'Torre Quemada', the burning tower, to the insane Inquisitor-General), but the *cuartel* (barracks) of the Holy Brotherhood is tumbling about the ears of the poor family it shelters; a fine stairway reduced to beggary, and traces of interior woodwork and carving reminding one of houses in the Edinburgh slums which still retain the vestiges of a noble origin in a staircase, a mantel-piece, or a window-moulding. The little banners suspended from the first-floor windows of these once aristocratic houses announce the occupations within; the sellers of wine adding a green branch to the modest sign. The bell-man is a drummer, sounding a rat-tat at the street corners and in the plazas to announce the market prices.

All the streets and, in fact, the town starts from the little hill on which the castle of the Counts of Villafranca stands looking out over the Bierzo. Being built after the taking of Granada it was never a fortified house. A fine building after the French model, with four solid corner towers and interest-ing ironwork still remaining, it crowns its small hill at the head of the other patrician houses with much dignity. Old plans within the house show extensive ornamental gardens after the pattern of Versailles, but even this arrow from home failed to avert the savagery of the French soldiers who harried the Bierzo, burning here thirty-one villages. There remain now a few cannons and chains, a gun, a drum in the parish church, and one wing of an ancestral castle habitable for a quiet country gentleman.

Hints of the roughness and hardness of a medieval pilgrim-age survive like battered belfries in insignificant corners. The tiny sanctuary of Santiago, now abandoned save of its shadows, had a door of pardon, through which those too ill or exhausted to go farther might pass and gain the fruit of their 'intention'. The row of weavers' houses fast against the steepness of the mountain cliff—the highway laborious and difficult still, though the narrow climbing bridge has been widened above its arches—once sold cloth to travel-worn pilgrims. What a caravan of human hope and credulity and rascality climbed that bridge into the mountain pass! A roomy old hostel for pilgrims has a much older carving built into its walls. Like the pebbles dropped one by one by prisoners in the tangled woods of fairy tales one picks up faint prints of an earlier faith and history.

The interchangeable B and V of this part of the country has an odd effect in the parish church. Entering the sacristy with the priest I was a little startled to read above a side door 'Bestuario', to be reassured by our guide who explained it as 'Vestuario', the room in which the priests vested themselves for the office. Bierzo itself is often written Vierzo.

But it is not from Villafranca, clasped in the mountains, that one gains best the vivid beauty of the Bierzo, but rather from the open valley in some situation like the royal monastery of Carracedo. The government Colony of Agriculture with its Oriental-shaped wells occupies what must have been the rich lands of the monastery. Travelling over the valley with the mountains rising from all sides is like journeying over the floor of a sunny lake from island to island coloured with sun and fruit. From every side the mountains give back from the warm sunny garden flowing with clear rivers, its climate like a golden wine cooled in snow.

But the royal monastery of Carracedo (of which Morales says that mention is made in a letter of St. Bernard), built from the ruins of the Roman city Bergidum (of which only earth-mounds remain), shares the fate of those vanquished by war and time. 'More like the ruins of history than its monument.' Of the outside walls four miles square, and the buildings magnificent as the wealth and power of its Order, there remain only the chapter-house and archive chamber and, most rare and interesting, the domestic Romanesque chambers of Doña Sancha, daughter of Queen Urraca, who repaired in 1138 the monastery which King Bermudo had built (in 990) for his sepulchre. This royal lady, on going a pilgrimage to Jerusalem, met St. Bernard on her homeward journey and was, through him, the means of bringing to Spain the Cistercian order of which this monastery of Carracedo was one of the principal foundations. The delicate colonnade of the balcony, like a doe caught in a wood, is almost choked in the jungle which was once a garden, but the chamber is in good preservation and of a very beautiful Gothic vaulting. Little by little the monastery stone is being stolen and its sculpture defaced by theft. Early sculptured figures are built into the wall. The museums of León and Madrid have preserved others. Astorga has its share. The base of the fountain at Villafranca came from its garden. The happy valley has legend echoing about it and has been greatly beloved. Borrow thought it one of the loveliest landscapes in Spain. Ford[1] became eloquent on its streams and fruitfulness. The Parsifal legend lives in its mountains. A readable little book (*Por Tierras de León*, by Padre Morán) gives a pleasant picture of customs surviving in the hidden villages of El Bierzo and the mountains which divide it from the Kingdom of León. How pagan customs still survive. How in the mass of Christmas night a circle of satiric songs is still

[1] Richard Ford, the early nineteenth-century traveller in Spain, whose witty and exhaustive guide-books are delightful reading and company.

sung by the women and girls, in which are incorporated out-standing comic happenings of the year. How the rosary in some high village contains an intercession—'For those who must confide in a frail plank for safety'.

Yet even in the Bierzo every evening in the bare upper room of the telegraph operator we listened to news from home, saying farewell only, when, carried by wireless, Big Ben struck the hour of midnight, and on the instant, beneath the window, in the street full of the sound of rippling waters, the Sereno raised his cry: 'Twelve o'clock and a quiet night'.

Chapter Thirteen

SAHAGÚN

Over a *terreno* spun out as fine as its atmosphere, the colour of its heaven thrice refined by sun, rain, and wind, its clouds stretching towards the distant mountains like swimmers in a tranquil water, above the silhouette of a sad-coloured town, lying flat and extended, with roads leading to it like brittle threads across the stubble lands of León, rise the solemn towers of Sahagún. They give the air of a city to a small Leonese town, unique in Spain, the first Romanesque towers built of brick in that country.

After Medina del Campo and its brick castle, one is prepared for dignity and beauty in a brick building. The north of Italy and the early Christian churches in Rome have these brick towers, and the sincerity and graciousness of the humble material used to so fine an architectural design is one of the pleasures of early Italian building. In a brick country, where the houses are built of sun-dried clay, and, in the high warm sun of Castile, sink into the insignificance of earth-mounds in the daytime, the rosy baked brick of the fine towers of Sahagún glows and flames at evening like that of some early and noble cathedral. San Tirso with its quadrangular tower and pillared windows above the beautiful Romanesque apse; San Lorenzo, more unusual, more solitary, with its tiers of windows and its bells, its three apses of brick and its sombre tower.

Of the 'Cluny of Spain' (the Abbey of San Benito) there is little more left standing than of the Cluny of France. A small habitable part of the monastery has been enclosed by a religious order, and the tombs of the Kings are now 'en clausura'. Something of the ambition and area of the notable foundation can still be gathered from its gateway and clock tower, its interior beauty from museums and chronicles.

'*The high altar is the largest, I believe, which there is in Spain, since it is sixteen feet long. It is entirely covered with plates of silver of very old workmanship, which with chasings and figures of Saints in half-relief make a rich frontal. It was ordered to be made by King Alfonso VI*' (MORALES).

The row of capitals in León museum, and the two lovely marble figures of Our Lord with the Evangelists, and The Virgin, Our Lady of Sahagún, in Madrid museum, show what was the delicacy and accomplishment of the sculptured decoration. Fragments of carving and ornament cling to the diminishing walls, and in the church of San Lorenzo the basin for holy water (itself the base of a marble column) stands on two capitals of marble of superb carving, and of date and workmanship similar to those in León museum, which must have come from the abbey. The State road now passes under the old gate of the monastery, which makes thus a triumphal arch to the lands and mountains of León.

Historical personages knew Sahagún and passed that way. Kings withdrew to the abbey and were buried there. Pedro the Cruel[1] first saw María de Padilla at Sahagún. San Juan de Sahagún spent himself as peacemaker in the vendettas at Salamanca; and another Pedro, of humbler and kinder station, Pedro Ponce, invented here his system of teaching deaf mutes.

'*The other notable Spaniard, of industry almost incredible if one had not seen it, is he who taught the dumb to speak by means of a perfect art which he himself invented. He is the Friar Pedro Ponce, monk of the order of San Benito, who has taught to speak two brothers and a sister of the Constable and now is teaching a son of the Justicia of Aragón, and it seems a greater marvel because of the profound deafness which has been the cause of their not speaking. Thus he talks to them by signs, or writes for them, and they reply in speech, and also write consecutively letters and other things*' (MORALES).

It was in the town of Sahagún, little visited save by an occasional architect, that the limitations of our own speech caused perplexity to a little Pedro Ponce of to-day. To be an artist, seated in a street, is to be at the mercy of any roving urchin big enough to look over one's shoulder, and to see a small crowd collected like a scrum at Rugby football in a quiet corner is to divine the presence of a seated artist. In the shadow of San Tirso a street door opened upon such a scene, and one of those comely patient faces (perhaps one of the

---

[1] Pedro the Cruel, 1350–1369. At one time friend and ally of the Black Prince, whom he was considered to have betrayed. Was involved in constant civil war. Son of Alfonso XI. María Padilla, mistress of Pedro the Cruel, whose apartments in the Alcázar at Seville are still shown.

most agreeable among the types of Spanish physiognomy) of the middle-aged mother looked out on the group, and then began a grave and reasonable explanation.

'This poor man who cannot speak! That is a sad thing, not a thing to make fun of. If he could reply to you it would be different, but now he sits like the deaf and dumb and you should not be unkind to him. He is like the dumb animals who are helpless because they cannot complain.'

Kind little mother of Sahagún! 'Hablamos poco, pero entendemos más!' (We speak little, but we understand more!) and we are not dumb in another tongue than Castilian. Speech being such a strange divider, courtesy is a fine and flexible bond, but Sahagún is still concerned about our speech.

In the fonda we all eat round a common table. To-night we are early and our only companion is a well-to-do peasant. As we seat ourselves we hope, as politeness demands, that his food will be acceptable to him. Having returned the compliment he is free to expand. He implores us with great simplicity not to be mortified that we speak Castilian so haltingly. He, of all Spaniards, is able to understand and sympathize with our dilemma, *buena fortuna*; for more than most he is accustomed to hearing bad Spanish spoken, since in fact in his población there is a Portuguese gentleman, his landlord, who speaks Spanish *very* badly! But this is the sympathy of the cautious. Little 'Pedro Ponce' has a further concern. Such a pleasant gentleman, capable of drawing all the stones in San Tirso and all the weeds in the roof; possessed of so many entertaining things which he brings out of bottomless pockets, and yet he cannot talk!

'*No puede usted hablar?*' (Cannot you talk?)

No! it is true! The gentleman makes sounds but cannot talk.

House of the Guzmans, León

The Eagle's Nest, Cuenca

'*Es fácil! Oiga usted!*' (It is easy, listen!) he explains very clearly to the gentleman. ' "*Hombre!*" Now say "*Hombre!*" ' '*Hombre!*' repeats the gentleman, quite plainly, to the delight of 'Pedro Ponce' who had never imagined it would be so easy to be a missionary and a pedagogue. '*Hombre, Hombre!*' He dances up and down. '*Más fuerte! Más fuerte!*' (Louder! Louder!)

God prosper you, little Pedro of the kind heart! Spain will not lack for men of benevolence while your race inhabit its pueblos.

The Alcalde of Sahagún is the most courteous of officials. There is talk in the Ayuntamiento of a museum to guard the treasures which are discovered from time to time. For notable artificers worked at Sahagún in the great days of San Benito. Juan de Arfe worked a *custodia* (tabernacle for the host) which is treasured in the Ayuntamiento together with a bronze handbell and a beautiful sixteenth-century embroidery from the abbey. The *custodia* is a very lovely and intricate piece of artificer's work. The delicate Gothic figure of The Virgin and Child in the centre, the tiny silver pinnacles with their sheltering saints, the kneeling angels, the worked border of the tabernacle and the *custodia*, produce a very lovely and precious object, and the figures of the Pasos in the long vaulted chamber of San Lorenzo suggest that once a good sculptor lived in Sahagún. The recumbent Christ, the three Maries, the Descent from the Cross, and the Christ in the Church itself recall the sincerity of emotion and lofty feeling which one associates with the master of Valladolid, Gregorio Hernández, and his school.

It is an unfastidious place, the Plaza, with its excellent Spanish habit of raising the first floor upon a colonnade and thus giving shelter from sun and rain to those whose business

E

is with the market or shop below. The constant passage of saddle beasts, of riders and flocks, gives to the streets the appearance of country roads which have somehow become entangled in a town. Old women sit in charge of pimientos and melons. Fresh fish comes by the train. On the pavement outside the door of the Ayuntamiento an excited group of boys and youths line up on each side of a dead vulture lying 'displayed'. The 'town's father' stands between the marble pagan columns which support his town hall. 'Who has killed it?' he asks, and as we turn from Sahagún we see a small boy come to the front to claim his reward.

Chapter Fourteen

ASTORGA

It passes as one of the unprogressive towns of Spain, its streets paved with what the Scots call 'kidney-stones', and only wide enough for the narrow ox-cart of the north to creak its heavy way through to the several plazas which still keep their open-air markets. One knows there will still be as many beasts as folk coming in to the plazas when one sees the uneven cobbled floors held down by crossing blocks of granite under the knob-headed acacia trees, and the rings fixed into the pavement for tying up saddle mules and donkeys. If one wants to watch a serious hard-bargaining market of country hand-made implements, pottery, and produce, one can yet find a fit setting in Astorga under the amusing little Renaissance town hall in the Plaza Mayor. Not too fine for its association with the market, it still keeps about its expression an air of whimsicality like a sagacious wide-breeched old Maragato itself. Above, two members of that now vanishing indigenous race, a Maragato and a Maragata, strike hours and record history, and all round the houses of the plaza support themselves on arcades. The bakers with enormous flat round loaves—'as hot as July, Señora!'—sit beneath the acacia trees, their white bread bought early and stowed away in saddle-bags by the country people. Avalanches of wooden implements slide on the cobbles—wooden yokes are stacked high—clogs laid in rows, *trillos* (threshing-sledges, their under sides teased with nails) are stacked like playing-cards; flat-pronged wooden forks and spades for tossing grain stand like tent poles. Sacks of madder glow in the sun. There are no factory-made articles visible. Pots are spread beneath the church door. In and out push the country people, their donkeys looped to their arms, an occasional Maragato, dressed like the Spaniards in the 'Surrender of Breda', as noticeable as an ancient Turk in modern Europe. This strange race, occupying a territory four miles square, with ancient customs (some, especially in wedding ceremonies, Jewish), and an elaborate and costly dress, rich as a Dutch burgher's, is passing and being absorbed as their language already has passed. With a reputation for being hard-fisted and wealthy many are now establishing themselves as fishmongers in Madrid, leaving the fame of their 'honour to death' in the old carrier days, to survive them in the country.

'Astorga was a Roman Colony and held Chancellery, being head of all the Province of Asturias, which was then more extensive than now, and gave it its name. On this account Pliny might call it a "magnificent city" rather than for the magnificence of its situation' (MORALES).

[112]

Like Lugo on the plain, it holds a position of control. Through Astorga passed the great military roads, four to Braga, two to Zaragoza, one to Tarragona, and another to Bordeaux. As at Lugo, too, one knows the weight of the wind which travels over the plain, by observing how the slates are tied down by stones on the chimneys outside the walls.

A fine cathedral is one of Astorga's possessions, and perhaps the most amazing bishop's palace that was ever built (by the modern architect Gaudí), being, in fact, so much too much of a palace for a bishop that the present bishop of Astorga could not be induced to live there. A palace, *muy macarrónico!* is the judgement of the cautious.

The really splendid national monument of its medieval walls, built so solidly for service from the Roman ones, have accommodated themselves, though but a portion of them is left, as well to the use of paseo and alameda as to the uses of ancient defence. On them one faces the magnificent extent of hill country within its range. Scotland has equally impressive piling of earth and granite; but not the expanses of rolling hillside or warm heat of soil. As the mountains raise the horizon to the variable sunlight, their summits uplifted in the serene blue vapour of distance, and the orange of the stubble-lands giving the landscape its last likeness to England, the 'magnificence' of Roman Astorga might even be extended to its situation.

The Memoirs of Baron de Marbot contain a curious reference to this unfamiliar town. 'Just as the corps of Soult and Ney were marching past the Emperor outside Astorga, cries were heard from a great barn. The door was opened and it was found to contain 1000 to 1200 English women and children, who, exhausted by the long march of the previous days through rain, mud, and streams, were unable to keep up with the army and had taken refuge in this place. For forty-eight hours they had lived on raw barley. Most of the women and children were good-looking in spite of the muddy rags in which they were clad. They flocked round the Emperor, who was touched by their misery and gave them lodging and food in the town, sending a flag of truce to let the English general know that when the weather permitted they would be sent back to him.'

Chapter Fifteen

ZAMORA AND SAN PEDRO
DE NAVE

ZAMORA

'The right bank for bread, the left for wine', say the Leonese of their deep river, and past the rectitude and starkness of the wheat fields, radiating their ominous ruddy heat, flows the noble flood of the Duero, with its following green, its soundless grey water, its reflections of beryl and shadows of amethyst, its slipping weirs and lines of water-mills standing out in the current, beneath the medieval bridge which carries the road into the town of Zamora—a subtle old bridge with eyes, which has offered a patient and incurious back to centuries of travellers.

How English one is after all! I am glad that I can 'stand up to' the bare magnificence of Castile in harvest, but how my eyes receive the tender greys and blues and amethysts of the river with its willows and silver poplars, and meet the wind flowing on the surface of the water with the joy of a greeting from home. Coming upon the shining river after the dry hot lands of harvest, one has a sudden understanding of the personality, as it were, of a great river, and of why in tropical heat its banks are crowded with worshippers, so completely does it change all life and all its visible appearance.

It is a mistake to suppose that Spain is a land of vivid colours. One goes to the Western Isles of Scotland for that. It is a country of light so intense that colours are subdued and obscured and simplified. A splendid and sombre glowing is what the cities return to the sunlight. Zamora, high on its backbone of cliff above the wide flood, one of the golden cities like Salamanca, looks like a city on a tidal creek within reach of some great outgoing water. The bagpipes of Zamora were Sancho Panza's fancy, but one comes to Zamora now for a fine Romanesque cathedral, a group of early churches and the famous tapestries. These are finely shown and preserved, peopling empty apartments with all mortal magnificence, Flemish imaginings of those pagan wars which live more credibly in tapestry than anywhere else.

'The tapestries are beautiful, but we shall never see them again', lamented an old washerwoman as we spoke of them. 'Once a year we were certain of seeing them, for they were hung in the cloister at Corpus, and we might all go in and have the treat of seeing them. Now only the visitors may look at them, for who among *us* can pay two pesetas? We shall never see them again.'

Whether the dome on Salamanca Cathedral will ever

emerge from its scaffolding and be seen again seems equally uncertain. So that the earlier gem of dome-building which distinguishes Zamora Cathedral gains an extraordinary value. If one walks across the bridge over the Duero and looks back from the end farthest from the town, this jewel of a cupola shines in its warm Byzantine beauty. By a happy accident, or by some sensitiveness in the architect, the late Gothic buttresses which support the apse appear from this point to complete the harmony of the beautiful dome, giving the illusion of a tiny but complete Eastern church like the old Metropolitan at Athens or the convent of Daphni on the road to Eleusis. The 'Lombard Tower' of Street's just admiration sinks in height and helps the illusion of something very primitive and early. From the opposite bank of the river, however, the tower rises again with its own history, lovely in colour, in strength, and simplicity, the noble early transept emerges, and the variety and distinction of the delicate jewel of its dome is disclosed in sunny detail. (The architects are even now busy disentangling the dome from some later masonry which obtrudes upon it, and it will soon stand clear on every side in its original intention and grace.) The transept, a compelling and noble piece of intellectual composition in simple stone masses, is as triumphant as Bach music, and the carving of the Virgin enthroned in the small tympanum introduces the delicacy of a pastoral interlude.

The little early churches for which one wanders below the walls among orchards and threshing-floors are full of beautiful ornament and detail. In the *barrio* (suburb) of Santiago stands the rough windowless chapel which gives its name to the suburb. It was before the altar of this humble place that the Cid was made a knight. One wide arch with columns vigorously carved encloses the sanctuary still, and the columns which once supported a second arch remain though the arch has fallen. Primitive and rough as the soldier who swore his oaths before its stone altar, it is now among the national monuments.

What a great outburst of animation accompanies the river! Throughout the harvest-lands attitudes of labour are classic, fixed, varying little. The Duero possesses wide green banks with sandy slopes, and a whole new variety of occupations follows its extended shores. Mill-wheels are punctual and dripping. Fishermen sink and float their three-cornered bronze nets into the green shadows of the island. Boats lie in the grey gloss of the lagoons. Mules and herds straggle down to drink and the sound of bells flows through the moving flocks like the irregular modulations of a stream. The washerwomen, kneeling along the margin, defend their rights from the Estremaduran shepherds with immemorial taunts.

'Ah . . . h Rosalita! you look like a black stork in the water!'

'Ah . . . h, vamos! Here is the gentleman working and we gaping like Portuguese sheep in the road!'

A long breath goes through the heated lands on the surface of the river. Against the luminous azure of the short summer dusk, black herds stand on the bleached sands under the mills; the weirs flutter white and the poplars hoard a generous shadow above water lucent and green as an agate.

SAN PEDRO DE NAVE

It was like the triumphant closing book of Doughty's *Dawn in Britain*, unexpected, stirring, glorious, the survival of this little church in the shelter of its green valley on the banks of the Eresma, safe from violation throughout the centuries of the Moorish occupation. What is it that makes these few sanctuaries (too humble and out of the way to attract spoliation) so moving and inspiring? After ten centuries they stand in their sincerity of building—the blocks of stone so honestly dressed that they remain one on the other without binding, in their nobility of proportion, their beauty of ornament, their pathetic antiquity, and their unexpectedness of situation. This, truly, is much to the artist. To the architect they are even more valuable. Within the church the priest handed me the monograph on this Visigothic treasure of the Eresma valley by Professor Gómez Moreno. I quote his closing words:

'To sum up, San Pedro de Nave represents perhaps the last phase of Spanish Visigothic art, with characteristics of its own, in which one traces local traditions—Latin teaching with echoes of the East, a faithful incarnation of the social vitality which Spain was unfolding, to be cut short at that point by the Arab invasion.'

We found it at last, searching for it across tracks and rough-cast roads between leagues of harvest country with the billowing and recessional of sea waves—the 'Nave' having no significance of 'ship' but being one of those cradles in the Sierras called 'Navas'. The high-roads of Castile divide a vast solitude. If, having left a trunk road, one comes upon the population of a great threshing-floor sunk down under the sunlight within some windless declivity, the sight is as startling as an apparition at midday, which passes before one on the light. A vision of the Kingdom of León in the year 1200 seems to rise to sight, some appearance which has been there all the time, but which some intensity of sunlight has defined and made visible.

These fair ghostly towns without shadows or noise in which black oxen tread as if for ever, in the sun-trampled alleys between the blond tents, lead one into dreams. Light lives here but no shadow. Insubstantial as a mirage, enchanted as sleep is the appearance of this heavy labour for bread. The toilers in this shadowless town seem to have lived there for ever, enchanted within a ring of alien mournful sunlight. The antique carriage of the sledge revolves over the threshing-floor like the rustling of wind in desolate grasses. So shadowless is this apparition that the labourers seem to have been placed on a background. The scarlet skirts of the women glow as if set by intention within these soft receding heaps without outline. Twenty oxen tread the corn, revolving in pairs like the wheels of some intricate engine. One woman seated on a sledge never raises her head. Her black kerchief shadows her face. The hands hidden in her lap give slight twitches to the reins which control her team of black bullocks. Her attitude, her stillness, are carried on and on by the heavy treading oxen. Would it ever stop? Had it ever stopped? Was it not there all the time, an apparition living only in certain strange sunlights?

The pueblos crouching behind the undulations of the land were silent as abandoned quarries. Rising and falling on a track like the bed of a stream, these ghostly harvest floors appeared and faded first on one side and then on the other. The sensation of journeying to the world's end went with one. Then the track precipitated itself down to a sudden green valley, a broad river, and the Visigothic church, rusty rose among the green. Colour changed. The scars in the hills were violet and blue, a slate country. The river showed green shores instead of flood. On a prominence above the opposite bank a tiny new church stands for those who cannot cross the flooded valley in winter, for the sanctuary of the Goths still serves five pueblos, three across the river. Sudden sweetness and cool after the fiery harvest-land surrounded the little church. A leafy mulberry-tree with an old woman sitting on a bench in the shade increased the tranquillity. For a moment we breathe the inviolable quiet and sweetness of the valley. The humility of the sanctuary, so old, so meek, touches the imagination. Through a yard, half farmyard, half garden, we find the priest's study. Two large doors opening straight on to the yard give air and light to a bare whitewashed room with slate floor. Against the wall is a table with some books and a short bench. There are two wooden chairs for visitors. That is all. The light comes from the open door, reflected light, giving the repose of a picture to the interior. The priest is young, with the good manners of Castile. Neither deprecating nor arrogant, he shares the dignity and repose of the valley sanctuary which he serves. He apologizes for his lack of English. 'You have no need to speak English here', we say.

'Hardly any need to speak Castilian!' he smiles quietly. 'No! there is not much snow here, nor intense cold. The danger is from the floods. You do not see much water in the river now, but in winter it is impossible to cross it for the torrent sometimes. I have been here fifteen years. Why this humble place was left untouched in the devastation? God protects the lowly, and the Moors were always afraid to venture into the mountains. This is a tiny Asturias here in Castile.'

'There is talk of a railway crossing the valley', we hint.

'No! the railway is to be carried over some short distance from this place, but it will be changed within a few years. The workmen and engineers will come to a village a few miles away, and then no doubt the valley will be much more frequented. You have seen it before that happens, as it has been for centuries.'

A tree untimely lopped is the figure most frequently used to lament the cutting short of the Visigothic architecture; and here again in San Pedro de Nave one wonders what would have developed, had larger and more ambitious work been attempted by those fine architects. Once more one wonders what it is which gives so tiny a building the dignity of something much more impressive in size. The columns of jasper like old stained ivory uphold their sculptured capitals —a gladiator, a knight, Daniel, the magi. The bands of ornament enrich the walls like the fine worked edges of a robe. The height of the vault, the low sanctuary, the three-fold apsidal chapels are all in character.

Of so much interest is this tiny church that Señor Lampérez devotes much space to demonstrating his conviction of its Visigothic origin. 'It is time now to classify the monument, and since from the Mohammedan invasion until the year 893 the district was not Christian, it must either be Visigothic and before the Mohammedan invasion or Mozárabe and after 893. A comparison of the elements in both epochs declares that San Pedro de Nave is Visigothic.

'1st. Because of the dressing of its stone, which is Roman. In the work of the tenth century this is somewhat form-less.

'2nd. Because of the ornamentation, which is abundant, rich, and similar to that of the seventh and eighth centuries and not to the rougher (barbarian) style of the time of Alfonso III.

'3rd. Because of the horseshoe arches, which are of the Visigothic and not the Mohammedan type.

'4th. Because of the epigraphy of the capitals, which is Visigothic and not Mozárabe.

'5th. Because of the *Art*, full of classical reminiscences (among others of the sarcophagus of Ecija), which did not survive to the tenth century.

'6th. Because of the material, which is of stone brought from a great distance and from across the Duero, proving the existence of a bridge, which did not exist in that century according to the description of the battle of Zamora written by El Masudi.

'From all which the learned critic of San Pedro de Nave (Señor Gómez Moreno) deduces that this church is of the last days of the seventh century or the first of the eighth, of the type of Greek Cross of the mausoleum of Galla Placidia in Ravenna, of Santa Comba de Bande, and of San Román de Hornija (although with the singularity of having the cross set in a rectangle), and of immense importance, because it marks a type of Visigothic church, until now solely and badly defined by San Juan de Baños, and displays a method of ornamentation distinct from the known Visigothic, in which one must recognize the prototype of the Asturian monuments of Ramiro I.'

We climbed to the rim of the world again and looked down into the valley before we went for ever into another century. The old woman was knitting beneath the mulberry-tree. The priest and his sister stood at the church door watching us, visitors from another planet, disappear over the edge.

Chapter Sixteen

SALAMANCA

'In these far climes it was my lot
To meet the wondrous Michael Scott;
A Wizard, of such dreaded fame,
That when, in Salamanca's cave,
Him listed his magic wand to wave,
The bells would ring in Notre Dame!'

Travellers' tales being not so much errors in fact as in application, the belief that Arabian learning had potencies at call was widespread when Alfonso the Wise (1252–1284), having rescued the University of Salamanca from an obscure and undignified position, encouraged there the mathematical sciences and the study of Arabic. The heavenly bodies, burning and secret, the mathematical symbols with an exactitude and power of their own, the tongue of the unchristian, surely the smell of brimstone lingered about the garments of those who meddled with such mysteries! So muttered the orthodox.

The mouth of Salamanca's cave, if it ever existed, was closed by Isabella the Catholic, and for the undergraduate of those times the chapel of Santa Bárbara held a sufficiently formidable aspect. For here, on the evening of his graduation as licentiate, he remained throughout the night, seated on the altar steps with his back to the altar, his knees against the upturned feet of the recumbent effigy of the founder, his book and candle upon the wooden covering of the tomb, under the observation of a beadle to whom the chapel interior was visible through the pierced Mudéjar[1] window from without.

There was a *viva voce* with alarms for the student, for though 'el gallo' (the cock) the patron of the candidate was allowed to crow his excellences aloud, there was also 'la gallina' (the hen) to proclaim to the examiners his misdeeds and shortcomings.

The perils of the night were doubtless remembered in another ceremony from which professors were absent. One of the first curiosities to attract the eye in Salamanca is the presence of red-letter names and anagrams on the façades of the public buildings. And they, too, have their story.

'*In the afternoon, after a homily, his companions carried the winner (in the examinations) on their shoulders, with torches and palms and thundering applause. One of the students, the master of the revels, mounted a ladder, from the top of which he harangued his companions, imitating and declaring aloud the defects of the professors to the accompaniment of violas and violins; then finally,*

---

1 Work of Moorish craftsmen under Christian rule.

with a paint made of red ochre, vinegar, and ox blood, painted on
the wall the name of the victor, with his coat of arms if he had one,
or suitable anagram or device, which remains on the façades of the
town until the present day.' (MARIANO DE SANTIAGO CIVIDANES,
Ceremonias y fiestas escolares.)

Some of them are as much as three centuries old, these
names of joyful students with paint brushes who became
(though not all, I fancy) bishops and viceroys, dating from
the days when the students, as history and the marble stair of
the university record, fought at least one bull on foot and
with lances, on the day of the rectorial election. The modern
Spaniard is inclined to deprecate a little the number of foreign
students who travelled to Salamanca for learning, but among
the multitude who lived there in the famous days of the sixteenth century there must have been many who did not
speak the Latin speech of Spain. Learning in those days re-
posed in scholars and not in books, and when travel was
most arduous people travelled everywhere.

'Apollonius the philosopher, simply to hear Hiarchus and
to see him seated on a throne of gold, teaching his disciples
the movements of the stars and their functions, traversed the
whole of Persia, overcoming the asperities of the Caucasus,
saw the Albanians and Scythians and a great part of India . . .
solely to listen to one man.' Craftsmen, pilgrims, crusaders,
mercenaries, explorers, students filled the highways of
Europe; and it was very much to induce the Spanish youth
not to wander to Paris for his learning that the importance of
Salamanca was emphasized in Spain.

There was but a wavering beginning possible to a university which had at one time to depend on the unstable patronage of kings like Pedro the Cruel, whose bright idea of
economy—to take a third of the churchmen's dues to pay

the professors—resulted in a pendulum movement of discontent, now clerics aggrieved, now professors; and it needed all the interlude of peace so cleverly maintained by Alfonso the Wise to bring stability and dignity to Spain's chief university. Within the university itself, backward and forward movements followed the brilliance of individual teachers, and it was fortunate for the prestige of liberal studies that they were later encouraged by the powerful Catholic Kings. Variations in the advancement of learning were bound to occur in the hubbub of some thousand brains at work. It was never certain what light would blaze and burn, and though, on the split in the Papacy, the Roman popes built a fortress for conservative theology in Salamanca (aiming thus a blow at Paris, which had hitherto held a monopoly in theological study, but which leaned to liberalism), though Salamanca turned away Columbus, the Copernican system was adopted without difficulty by the university, women studied at Salamanca, and a chair of music was instituted before such a thing was heard of even at Oxford (1313). After the summit there can be but descent, and by the very learning which Salamanca stood to teach her eminence became divided. Other universities were founded, and novelty has a savour. And though the student is reputed to have helped to pull his house of learning about his ears by riotous behaviour, bringing the university under the civil law and breaking the prestige of the university courts, it was finally the wars of succession and of independence, with their local storms round Salamanca, which held up the highways of learning. To-day Salamanca is a town with a university, with beautiful Plateresque architecture and great names echoing about it and the courage to rebuild its magnificent Plaza Mayor in a style becoming to a capital.

Heart of Spain, one thinks it, as one travels the day-long journey over the wide granary floor of Old Castile, a country of riders and horses, of high classic churches rising like ships against the sun, of roads leading to horizons, of lands rolling their green and golden waves to end in the sinking day. It is 'Parador' which is the most frequent name on the hostelries of the town, for man and beast come together across the 'lands' of Castile, and the rows of horses and mules tied at the stables fill the smaller plazas with animation. Its chief modern poet (Gabriel y Galán) was the poet of country and shepherds. (After the charming manner of modern cultivated Spain, he is set to preside over the new open-air library in the public garden of the city.) To tumble into Salamanca on top of four days of bull-fights and the biggest horse fair in Castile is to apprehend at sight the width of the lands stretching around it. The horses gathered on the hill are like an invading army. The Roman bridge, its advance across the river as unswerving as that of the legions, bears a day-long caravan of horses and riders, all suggesting expanses of country without towns, of the continuance of antique ways unconsidering of passing governments.

Regional dress and ornament have not yet been displaced in Salamanca.—'El charro' and his lady still carry many ounces of precious metal disposed in jewels and buttons about their ancient Castilian costumes, and to see a bride of the well-to-do farmer in her inherited ornaments is to look at a fine (and expensive) work of art.

'The first word the babies say in Salamanca is "Toros"', said our friend at the café, and Salamanca must rival Seville in its enthusiasm for the battle of the arena. Did not some scholar of its university recently announce in an article apropos of the bull-ring, that Fray Luis de León, the saint of

Salamantine professors, supported and voiced the appeal for the continuation of the bull-fighting among the students? Twenty-eight was the number of the bulls to be killed on these days of the Feria. Day after day the whole population of Salamanca arose from whatever occupation it followed and stampeded to the arena, to return in the same delirium of excitement. 'You do not care to see the bull-fight just once —as a very Spanish thing? Ah! there are sentiments here against it!' Our friend laid his hand upon his heart. 'But, Señores, what pretty girls! What Córdoba hats! *What bulls!*'

ESTILO PLATERESCO

When Gothic architecture reached a point in which its elaboration suggested over-ripeness and readiness to give place to some new structural invention, it is interesting to compare the final forms which it took in the various countries which it had dominated for centuries. The late-decorated or florid Gothic of France found little sympathetic in the English development. Instead, the English style suddenly broke away into the 'perpendicular', producing the beautiful English towers—Lincoln and the spire of Salisbury, and the peculiarly English fan-vaulting of King's College Chapel, Cambridge, Christ Church staircase, and Henry VII's Chapel—while for a period in Spain there flowered a style all of its own in which Renaissance motives were grafted on a Gothic structure, sometimes with a very graceful and delicate simplicity, sometimes so lavishly as to be hardly distinguishable from the most elaborate arabesque invention.

It was rather to play upon the severe Gothic rule than to supersede it, that the originator of the Plateresque style made experiment. 'After the death of Calixtus III (1458) a Catalan goldsmith of great repute, Pedro Diez, whom the Pope had summoned to Rome, returned to Spain and settled at Toledo. He entered the workshops of the cathedral and acquired such ascendancy there that Enrique de Egas, son of the master of works, came entirely under his influence. Although he had been brought up by his father in the pure tradition of Flemish Gothic, he nevertheless built at Valladolid the College of Santa Cruz in which the impress of the Italian Renaissance is very obvious. Thus we find a goldsmith, a *platero*, connected with the evolution of pointed architecture. Hence the term *plateresco* applied in Spain to the elegant and individual style of the reigns of Joanna the Mad and Charles V.' So Monsieur Dieulafoy, who writes with some expansion upon a period of architecture evidently sympathetic to him.

Very ductile is that golden stone of the North of Spain of which Salamanca is largely built, and very possible to work elaborately. Less so is the granite of Compostela, yet the elegance and richness of Plateresque style are both seen in the front of Isabella's hospital and the cloister of Santiago Cathedral. From Seville to Salamanca the new finesse worked upon austere traditions until a very beautiful page of architecture was written in Spain, mostly on civil buildings, town halls (as at Seville), universities, and convents (as at Salamanca), seignorial houses (as at Trujillo, León, Salamanca, Valladolid, the notable cities of Renaissance building). At its best there is nothing quite like it elsewhere than in Spain, though its influence spread to Portugal and to Flanders. It can be in turn severe, with only one slender line of decoration disposed upon a massive façade, or rich as an embroidered mantle or beaten silver as in San Pablo in Valladolid. In its latest stages, in the façade of San Marcos in León, it approaches, still lovely and ornate, with its rows of plaques and pilasters, more closely to other Renaissance developments than the purely Spanish.

One is always pleased to see it, its refinements having a peculiar value amid the gravity of Spanish architecture. The corner windows and carved escutcheons, the careful proportioning and disposition of the grilles on the house fronts, as in the house of the Guzmáns at León; the patios with contrary flexed arches like those of the 'House of the Shells' at Salamanca; the enrichment, panel by panel, of a considered space above a doorway, as in Salamanca University and various houses in its streets; the fretted balustrades in the cloisters of Santiago de Compostela and Segovia, the delicate flowering of stone ornament about windows, themselves the only break in a massive and severe façade; the House of the Momos in Zamora, produced a style in which the decoration becomes indeed a part of the integral design, springing from it and in turn producing it. It was a style which went happily with a certain dignity of living, lingering about old court towns and resorts of learning. Salamanca, with its wide humanistic appeal, must at one time have been wonderfully rich in these Plateresque buildings. Even now, names arrange themselves quickly in a list—The House of the Dead; the House of Monterey; the House of St. Teresa; the House of the Shells; the courts and doorways of the University and Minor Schools, all bear the gracious passing of this style upon their dignified fronts. The elegance and liberality and grace of Plateresque architecture were a pleasant setting for the Humanities and for the cultivated existence of the early Renaissance.

In Valladolid, that easy old capital, full of art and workshops and great names, Plateresque ran exuberantly. Even the one beauty left in the palace of Charles V where the saturnine Philip II first drew breath is a Plateresque window, and, though the genius of Herrera was to impose other scruples upon the town, some of the most sumptuously disposed of early church fronts are of the fashion. The fronts of San Pablo and San Gregorio are like rich mantles hung upon supports. The upper cloister of San Gregorio is more like a Moorish minstrel's gallery than that of a college of priests.

Seville built its Town Hall in this style, León its convent of St. Mark. The arrogance of the Conquistadores softened a little towards Plateresque in Trujillo; Zamora entertained it. Cáceres and Palencia considered it. It died without decay, happier than some other, and these, it may be, greater phases of art.

Chapter Seventeen

CUENCA

Tossed up on precipices, half old Edinburgh, half Mount Athos, within a rim of grey, tragic, and ashen hills like some fantastic and unhomelike landscape of the moon, Cuenca, after Calatayud, is the most singular city in Spain. Two rivers, deep sunk in abrupt and violent gorges, dividing at the base of a prodigious rock, cling about its foundations. Columns twisted by erosion march on the face of the precipices, heavy with vegetation like the pergola of some monstrous invention. To look over from the top is to look into the classic desert of art. In such a place Abraham for ever sacrifices Isaac. Poussin fills such rock escarpments with sunlight—strange, grey, burning with light! One peers over into the valley through the postern of St. John. From the valley beneath, locked with precipices, where the river lies deep and tranquil as a tarn (the only space open in the

[133]

tumult of piled and tumbling rocks), Martín Alhaja[1] the Christian shepherd led in the Christian army crawling on all-fours and covered with the skins of the sheep he had led out to pasture in the morning. Furtive, desperate, and secret, from the passage cut through the rock of the hillside one follows the sheep-track of the poor wise man who by his wisdom gained the city, and finds the real bed-rock of Iberia Dura.

From the depth of the valleys the hill formations seem to have been thrust up and built on high, continuing the lines of the real city in some singular caricature, fantastic edifices built upon a cliff. The high-storied grey houses are themselves partly of living rock. In the dusk it is impossible to say where rock merges into building. To climb and cross the high bridge of San Pablo where the monastery cliff locks the valley, and to enter the town at nightfall through the windings of the passage cut through the solid rock (dim and sinister as the cavern it really is) between the 'eagles' nests' of Cuenca and the enormous fortified house of Gómez Carrillo, is to recover, if one has a liking, many medieval thrills and apprehensions. For in the eagles' nests of Cuenca lived Torrealba the wizard—'Torrealba the licentiate, who in games of chance lost his money and in hazards of love his life'—brought to that high perch on the wings of demons from Valladolid to be major-domo to Carrillo, until the Inquisition required his attendance with explanations, and

---

[1] Martín Alhaja, a Christian shepherd who, in 1177, when Cuenca was besieged by Alfonso VIII, led his sheep outside the walls of the town apparently to pasture, but led them to Alfonso's army. The fleeces of the sheep, killed and eaten by the starving army, were then used as a disguise by the soldiers, and at nightfall what was apparently a flock of sheep returning, was in reality an army on all-fours, who, once within the city, took it by surprise and captured it.

he was seen no more. But now it is only abandoned houses which are so silent. The shadows of the palace retain neither dangers nor demons.

Beneath them, every step in the valley of the Huécar is of incredible picturesqueness. Convents tempting Providence and gravity stand on the verge of the precipices. No solemn ilex or cork oaks follow the river, but silver birch, alders, poplars, and hazels ripple at the bases of the grey chasms. High-storied and grey, with here and there a yellow house like the lichen stain on the limestone hills, with the colours of autumn dropping aureolin and gold upon the poplars and birches under the grey terraces of rock, Cuenca is altogether of the tone of her stricken and mournful hills. A grey day full of energy and piled with cloud is a fine wrapping for this city of high grey precipices and houses. But under no light or dark does the town lose the interest of its dominant and uncompromising shapes, and to see summer lightning playing upon the rim of the Gargantuan hill-pitcher which is its lodging, is to see a strange exile and grave for the end of Montezuma's race, the last of the Incas, 'Don Pedro'.

Along the sides of the strange green river valley of the Júcar, rocks stand like giants drawn up in line, stony and mournful, and from the 'hill of majesty', on which stands the sanctuary of St. Julian the Tranquil, one sees that the whole region is full of those fantasies of Nature, cyclopean anvils, statues of mournful gods half effaced by weather, capricious, improbable, immense, or majestic; and farther in the Sierras outlines of 'enchanted cities', with castles, steps, arches, and streets, sculptured by water, wind, and snow, a genial gigantic fantasy of Nature and of flowers.

'If a man with all the world before him to live in were to choose to live in Castile', says Pío Baroja, 'he would inevitably choose to live in a city. If the north of Spain were his choice, he would as surely elect to live in the country. All the history of Castile is the history of convents and castles.'

The old palaces climb the steep street to the castle, and it is here, on the great thrust of rock which cleaves apart its two deep valleys, that Cuenca stands out in some likeness to its past importance, a city easily to be imagined as full of commerce, pride, and art, with a tale of great names equalled by few cities in Spain. The town on the rock, with its old and decayed fortifications, is amazingly silent. No shops, no markets, no high road! The heavy bulk of the seignorial houses overshadows the narrow and tortuous lanes with silence and chill. How massive the long wall of the house of Mendoza whose lower stories are cut in the rock! How high and secret with its small guarded windows! The narrowest possible footways wind beneath the most massive palace walls, and in the secretive and wary appearance of the streets one forgets to notice how good the Ayuntamiento building is, or that the town possesses one of the three cathedrals of New Castile.

The 'English cathedral of Spain' has some of the finest Renaissance ironwork in that country of good blacksmiths, for commerce was once good and money abundant in the 'forgotten city of Castile', and it was worth the while of a first-rate craftsman to attach himself to the Cathedral of Cuenca.

It is still to the Plaza in the high rock town that the bull-fighter is carried shoulder high after a successful fight. It is still the Plaza which is barricaded for the cow-baiting which follows the *feria* (fair), and from which the fireworks are set off. But it is in the level streets below the old town that expansion is carried on, and to these that the life of the mountains travels down the valleys to the city and its paradores. Here, as in Salamanca, the peasants still wear the regional dress, black small-clothes with silver buttons; white, scarlet, or blue stockings with grey gaiters, and hemp sandals laced about the ankles; a wide body scarf stuffed like a gnome's; black velvet jacket or blue blouse, and a black head turban knotted at one side with a long hanging end.

Behind the Sierras of Cuenca it is a forest and mountain country. The ox disappears as a carrier. Caravans of charcoal-burners travel down to the town. The logs are brought from the hill forests by mules, yoked with a wide wooden yoke from which hangs a hook to steady the long pine trunks, and the timber is floated down to the Tagus. All the animation of the town is about the entrances to the posadas. The big dim yards are full of carts. Groups of peasants sit on the mounting-blocks within the wide doors. Mules and donkeys follow their masters about like dogs. It will be long before the Ford car can take possession of this mountain country, but if it ever does, what animation and interest will disappear from the streets of these ancient Castilian towns with their entertainment for man and beast!

There is a good fountain in the public garden in the newer town, carved by Marco Pérez, of a woodman of the Sierras, sinewy and watchful, his axe and pine-cones in the crook of his elbow, the heads of wolves at the fountain base. That lean and arduous forest life is all there, finely imagined and executed. The peasant, alert to the last limit of his muscular endurance, the trickle of mountain water, the axe for life and defence, the wolves!

I look at him with interest to-day, for does not the daily paper dispute the case of the peasants at Henajares, the village which it takes a letter three days to reach, where you cannot see the world for the pine-trees and can hardly find the village, though you journey there on horseback. These peasants, such woodmen as sit lean and alert on Marco Pérez's fountain, have suddenly 'seized the land' in which they work. The bishop, the alcalde, and a notable lawyer of Cuenca have set off into the mountains to hear causes and administer justice. I look at the man on the fountain, hearing the echoes of the quarrel in the forest. 'We work always and some one else takes all the gain.' 'Why when we work do we never get any farther on? The land is ours, our work has earned it.' Even in the far forest where you cannot see the world for pine-trees these things are happening, and that in Spain.

Chapter Eighteen

SANTIAGO DE COMPOSTELA: I

SANTIAGO DE COMPOSTELA

Atlantic weather with its prevalent moisture visits these hills of Galicia. Clouds and energetic skies are everywhere among the beauties of Spanish landscape, for the sky, even in Southern Spain, is not always of unclouded blue, and in the neighbourhood of any of the Sierras their chief company is the heavens in majesty. In Galicia it seems as though the exhalations which rise amid the hills take with them also something of their colour. Mobile, gathering, dispersing, the ethereal hills are built anew every day above long valleys like the beds of lakes drained of everything save the light.

Deep, heath-coloured country and granite mountains guard the hills of Compostela with its shrine and church of Santiago (St. James) the Apostle, a place of pilgrimage, an ascent, with bronze bells telling the hours of centuries and of history. As the sunlight and bright wind open distances on the surrounding hills, roads are visible on their slopes converging from all sides to the hill of Santiago, beautiful for situation. White glimpses faint in summer heat, paths broken by declivities to reappear higher among the heather, one has only to enter Compostela from any road over the hills to see how often the towers of her cathedral appear through openings across the valleys long before the streets of the town give their certainty to the wayfarer.

Compostela, with its guard of hills, once the most famous shrine in Europe, with roads trodden to it from every quarter by the feet of pilgrims, was once further gathered up into walls on its own eminence like a fortress. To-day it remains compact, its centre heavily magnificent, its streets arcaded with strong granite porticos, its domestic architecture unpretentious, here and there the sombre mass of a religious house shuttered and blind, with valerian and borage growing on its walls as on a forsaken grave, taking emotion from the volume of sunlight which envelops its immobility with shadows. Below the hill on every side are villages attached to Compostela by the wavering thread of a rivulet. Where water is abundant and fluent one expects animation about its confluences, and shadowed by little granite calvaries the washerwomen kneel and wash.

In the poorer part of the town modest streets of houses with cockle-shells carved above the doors announce the ancient inns for pilgrims, and Isabella's guest-house and sanctuary the royalty of demeanour of that high-spirited lady towards the wayfaring Catholic. For although three active streams of life flow through Compostela—the youth of the University, the peasants surging up to the market-

The Cathedral, Santiago

Old Trujillo

place, and the activities of the cathedral—it is still the hospitality and interest of the shrine of Santiago which dominates them all. Legends stand like sentinels about the militant apostle. Fire-balloons float over the hills which proclaim the arrival of a group of pilgrims at his doors. One can tell the moment at which a pilgrimage mounts the great stair beneath the Porch of Glory by the explosion of bombs. Women working in the fields outside the town straighten themselves, and look up. The road watchman sitting in his stone hut and the shepherd on the hillside turn towards the breaking of flame in the sky. It is both announcement and fulfilment.

LA PEREGRINACIÓN

'How should I your true love know
From another one?'
'By his cockle hat and staff,
And his sandal shoon.'

I never had a mind to go on a pilgrimage except to the days of my youth that I might know whether the years condemn false hopes or low fears, and only a few times in Europe have I met genuine wayfaring pilgrims, each time very old people, regarded with an indulgent smile by the officials from whom they asked their way, as people given to occupations a little behind the times. But the Tower of London once made a steady revenue from the tax of sixpence imposed on every English pilgrim who wore the cockle-shell badge for a pilgrimage to St. James overseas. Ophelia knew it. Helena's disguise was the palmer's habit for Saint Jacques le Grand. The Wife of Bath had added a pilgrimage to Saint Jaime in Galice to her record; and the polyglot hymn of the early pilgrimages shows the popularity of St. James's shrine in the Low Countries:

'*Herru Sanctiagu*
Got Sanctiagu
eullreja
esus eja
Deus adjuva nos.'

It is from the point of view of the town which receives the pilgrims that one has watched them come up to the shrine of the Apostle for many past months. For though the great pilgrimage ways of Europe are travelled no longer and St. James is now a Spanish saint, since the station is a long way off, the town of Compostela on a hill, and the diligences stop outside, there is still the illusion as the processions of pilgrims come to the Pórtico de la Gloria that they have come on foot; and though the pilgrimages have more the air of a Sunday-school outing than a spiritual effort, they are still interesting, the ceremonies dignified and adequate, the hospitality of the town attractive. Isabella's handsome idea of a guest-house for pilgrims, with its beautiful Plateresque balcony and interior chapel and courtyards, witnesses to the difficulty of housing the multitudes who travelled over the pilgrimage roads to Compostela. So many came that the inns of the town could not suffice for accommodation and the pilgrims often slept in the cathedral itself. Probably indeed, the origin of the giant censer, *el botafumeiro*, was hygienic, for braziers of incense are said to have burned all night in the cathedral in medieval times, and an ancient cross upon the parapet of the church is shown as the place where the pilgrims washed and hung their travel-worn clothes to dry, change of clothing being provided by the archbishop.

No one washes clothes there now or hangs them on the cross. If the pilgrims are country folks come in by the early morning diligences you will meet the women thronging the shops where the coloured silk squares are sold with which they cover their heads, and the men in the smithies leaving their sickles and knives to be sharpened, or waiting round the menders of umbrellas or farm implements who sit in the markets. This until the time for the cathedral dignitaries to receive the pilgrimage. Then the pilgrims assemble in the Plaza and ascend the stairs to the Porch of Glory. Banners are carried and sometimes the saint of the village, and often the Galician pilgrimage comes with the *gaiteros* (pipers) playing them in. The houses of the town hang festival cloths of red and yellow on the balconies, and the pilgrim song is played by the town band. Fireworks and bombs and balloons announce the arrival of the procession at the cathedral doors.

Within, there is the welcome by the canons, mass, and a sermon from the Archbishop, a visit to the shrine of the Apostle and the censing of the whole congregation by the botafumeiro. This heavy silver censer (six feet high as it swings) is carried like the grapes of Eschol on a staff borne on the shoulders of two men. It is attached to a rope and pulley pendent from the central dome, the pilgrims throng to the transepts across the entire breadth of which it swings, the dignitaries emerge with an extraordinary effect of colour from the Coro, and having paced the ambulatory halt in the transept. Two very primitive bassoons and some horns begin the wailing, lulling, swaying melody of the pilgrims' hymn, and seven men raise and swing the botafumeiro. The arc of silver (with its smoke circling about it like swarming bees) cuts the gloom of the vaulting from transept to transept. It is a strange scene in the dim church—the upturned faces of the pilgrims; the boys holding the tall candles in silver candlesticks; the smoke and fragrance of the censer filling the dome; the brave Titian reds and gold and purple of the ecclesiastics making credible at last the sombre and elaborate gilding of altar and sanctuary; the image of Santiago in his cape of jewelled gold, motionless in the tabernacle, and the reedy ancient cradle-song of the botafumeiro finding its way through centuries to the echo and gloom of the aisles.

THE NATIONAL OFFERING

From the dominance of Compostela as a place of pilgrimage it became greatly prosperous in commerce, being one of the first towns of Northern Spain to acquire independence as a township. Its bishop Gelmírez maintained a private navy: and the history of the building of its cathedral—with the central motive of interest in the shrine—is the record of the rising or passing of architectural styles, proportioned to the ambitions of churchmen and the prosperities of trade. This beautiful Romanesque cathedral is one of the disguised Gothic churches of Spain; so re-made and re-decorated as to its outer walls after Churriguera that one seems to have wandered through another door and mistaken the church when the antique and undisturbed Romanesque interior finally receives one. Something of the unfamiliarity of impression (to English eyes) left by a Spanish cathedral of familiar architectural invention, comes from an unaccustomed lighting (the desire, it may be, to preserve the luxury of quiet for the eye from the volume of sunlight out of doors). There is no clerestory. The light flows through the aisles on the level of the lower windows, except where a flood descends from the dome above the Coro. So that the dimness of the nave becomes part of the architectural intention, as it were, and darkness deepens to a colour. Something, too, a little ancient and immobile clings to the arrangement of a Spanish cathedral attached still, one imagines, to some monastic idea. The central position of the Coro seems to shoulder the congregation outside, and the nave appears a little purposeless. Yet there are times (one such being that of the National Offering) when the very emptiness of the nave gives moment to the grouping of ecclesiastics before its altar. Some effect from very long ago seems to be 'staged', as it were, from an older Spain than the present, from ceremonial very established and unchanged, from something even deeper still, it may be, the desire to leave them unchanged.

'Now tell me,' said a Spanish architect, 'would you *like* a Spanish cathedral to be like an English or a French one? Oh yes! I know that to come into one of our cathedrals gives a French architect the vertigo! But would you like Santiago to be so cold, so empty?'

It is on the day of the Ofrenda Nacional that I am in accord with the feelings of the Spaniard.

From the time when it seemed as though Spain must make visible the wealth of the Indies, those gilded sanctuaries, now so deep and sombre in tone, stole within the severe Gothic shell. When empty of ceremony the pillars and angels and clouds have the effect of an over-elaboration of preposterous glories. But the deep glow from the ornate gilding takes its relation fitly enough when the tapers are lit and the purple and ruby and gold vestments group and pass and shimmer and live before the altar, as a rich shrine for a very splendid pomp. Nothing less magnificently glowing could support the weight of colour which fills the sanctuary on the day of the National Offering and the Feast of the Apostle.

[145]

When Sancho Panza tempts Don Quixote to abandon knight-errantry and become a saint, since even kings visit the shrines of saints and he never heard of any august person taking much notice of a knight-errant, he might well have had Santiago in his mind. During Apostle's Week (the offering is made on St. James's Day) pilgrims surge up from the country literally in thousands, singing as they approach. Highly placed officers of the Spanish army collect in the town. Ecclesiastics gather daily. Every day another coloured uniform or cloak is added to the brightness of the streets. Festival hangings shine in the cathedral: the silver altar is uncovered; candles fill dark recesses with their mystical flowering. Through the whole town a deeper colour, a quicker life, passes like a wind, to culminate in the ceremony and magnificence of the Apostle's Day.

One day, at sundown, a line of cavalry officers covered with dust ride up the arcaded streets, each with drawn sword or the banner of St. James in his hand (the hilt of the banner stuck in his boot), and dismounting at the cathedral steps kneel and kiss the hand of the Archbishop and place their banners before the altar. For Santiago, the caballero and militant saint of legend, gives his name to the chief military religious Order of Spain, and it is the privilege of the Knights of Santiago to accompany the National Offering to his shrine. Again the quality of some unaltering and very ancient outlook seems to stir the surface, some deeply homogeneous quality of the Spanish mentality—ecclesiastics, people, soldiers, in equal parts of the ceremony.

Fairs of horses and cattle are taking place in the town, pageants are making ready for the streets, fireworks for the evening. Within the cathedral the transepts grow dim, as colour slowly amasses within the shining sanctuary. Fifteen bishops in purple and gold vestments, with gold and silver mitres, and with their attendant canons, set themselves within the chancel; while the Knights of Santiago, robed in the white cloak and red cross of their Order, await the arrival of the Infante with the King's offering at the Porch of Glory. He comes as a pilgrim up the pilgrims' stairway and is conducted by his companions in the Order to the sacristy to be robed. The Mass advances to the Gloria—the botafumeiro swings above the heads of a vast congregation, its little reedy cradle-song on the horns sounding with a naïve familiarity like a child's voice singing a hymn at a coronation; the moment for the offering arrives.

Though the Spaniard may at times pay the penalty of those who go their own way through the changes of history, there are moments when he is justified—of effect at any rate. Titian and Veronese come nearest to the suggestion of glowing colour now moving in ceremonial. The red-gold sanctuary with the silver altar and the archaic figure of the Apostle in his jewelled cape of gold; the light of tapers absorbed, as it were, rather than reflected in the gilding; fifteen gold-mitred and vested bishops seated on either side of the altar, servitors with tall silver croziers and candlesticks, are all grouped and motionless, and between the choir and the sanctuary there advance two by two the Knights of Santiago, each now with his long white velvet train fastened to his shoulders. The Infante kneels with the offering, and each knight receives a posy presented on the enormous silver cockle-shell salver which carries the vestments of the Archbishop. The dignitaries leave the altar, their sudden emergence into the crowded aisles so vivid that the colours seem to live of themselves in the gloom, and passing down to the sunshine of the Western Door descend the pilgrims' stair. And now, there is still another ceremony to add to those of the Apostle's Day. For in the outer wall of the cathedral lodge eight giants invisible for all the rest of the year (large wicker frames for bodies, papier mâché for their eighteenth-century heads). On the day of the Apostle's vigil they come out of their cupboard, dance round the Plaza three times, and then, accompanied by dwarfs and two pipers in yellow, promenade the streets of the town. And on the Apostle's Day? The gorgeous stream of dignitaries has passed out into the sunlight of the Plaza—authority, as it were, has looked the other way; and again the giants emerge, this time into the cathedral, with their two pipers in yellow, piping boldly through the aisles. The sanctuary is empty. The tapers are still lighted before the image of the Apostle. No living person is there. The two smaller giants enter the sanctuary (the six tall ones standing to attention outside), dance solemnly on the empty carpet before the Apostle, and then all retreat, and, making the ambulatory of the whole cathedral, go back into their cupboards until the Apostle's Day of the succeeding year. It is like an imagination of Hans Andersen: the fantasies after the pageant, the strange image and the lit candles in the deserted sanctuary, the giants popping in as soon as authority smiles and looks the other way, dancing their top-heavy minuet on the empty carpet and clapping back into their cupboards when the candles are put out. With this popular and very Spanish relaxation the ceremony of the National Offering is concluded.

Santiago: The Royal Hospital

Chapter Nineteen

SANTIAGO DE COMPOSTELA: II

MAESTRO MATEO

The figure of Maestro Mateo, burly and half legendary, is of the company which seemed to walk the world in the Middle Ages, the master-craftsman with tools on his back, knowledge in his head, and skill in his fingers, for whom kings and archbishops used to send when some chantry or tomb was to excel any before ever seen, when an altar or chapel must be gilded or carved, or a bishop's robes arranged in marble. If, being such a one, you could give to your generation some gift which no other could command, you were rightly and fortunately 'Maestro', and so Mateo!

There is not much more known of Maestro Mateo who built the Porch of Glory in Santiago Cathedral at Compostela than there is of Shakespeare. That he was French and came from the centre of Gothic sculpture at Toulouse is hotly disputed by the Spaniard. The record shows him to have come to Compostela in 1168, at the bidding of Don Fernando the King, to add the porch (possibly with the idea of enlarging the church) to the Cathedral of St. James the Apostle, and that he was content to live and work at Compostela for twenty years, bringing the company of heaven to welcome the devout on earth, and to carve his own robust figure among the docile monsters with folded paws who support the heavenly arches, to vouch for the integrity of his work before any maestro or craftsman who might pass by in later times.

In these days when art jumps into experiment and out again, this master of the twelfth century is a comfortable figure to think upon, settling down to his work on the Pórtico for twenty years. For there is danger in isolation only to the ill-nourished in knowledge and heart, and there was nothing starved or attenuated in the achievement of the Master of Compostela, the fame of whose intellect is so deeply established that peasants and pilgrims bring their children to rub their heads against that of the curly-headed Maestro (he being comfortably crouched on the floor at a child's height) to increase their mental powers, and little school children steal in after school, with the evening preparation before them, and say their prayers with one hand on Maestro Mateo's head, he being, for them and their needs, one of the most accessible saints of the Pórtico, a generous big brother among the holy.

And now criticism winds slowly about this legend. Was Maestro Mateo only the architect of the Pórtico and the Master of Works of the cathedral? Did he indeed carve any of the figures? Was he a sculptor at all? Are not three separate artists visible at work upon the porch? May not the smaller columns and even some figures have been brought from elsewhere and incorporated in the structure like the gems which stud the gold cloak of St. James in the treasury?

What is actually visible is a beautiful company gathered together in a heavenly dwelling supported at the head of a superb double stairway on three arches, up which the pilgrims climbed to the shrine of Santiago. From the head of the stair the sight of this company of the glorified first greets the pilgrim. A great central tympanum holds the majesty of the throne and the sinless ones round about it. At the feet of his Lord sits St. James the Apostle leaning on a palmer's staff; prophets and saints and angels are gathered upon the columns in lower places. Every lovely and honourable person upon whose witness the Christian Church was built has been drawn to this reunion. Once coloured and glowing and gilded it must have appeared indeed the Gate of Glory to the wayfaring pilgrim.

> 'I see them walking in an air of glory,
>   Whose light doth trample on my days;
> My days which are at best but dull and hoary,
>   Mere glimmerings and decays.'

The assumption that the Pórtico is the work of a single master has also presupposed that the work is a unity. But to examine the arches from outside this tradition is to find the very unusual beauty of the central arch with its tympanum and the column bearing the figure of the Apostle, a fact hardly to be explained by the work on the other figures of the Pórtico. The sculpture of this central and most perfect conception of the Gloria was certainly all by the hand of one man; and to find, in a remote corner of Spain, such a superbly finished carving at so early a date, of itself announces the presence in Compostela of one master of pre-eminent genius. Such happy originality and liveliness of conception justify the sober Street's 'one of the greatest glories of Christian art'. 'Blithe' is the word which springs to the mind at the sight of so lovely and candid a conception. So sweet and reposeful in character, of such variety in gentleness, of such tender and subtly considered manipulation are these figures with eyes not fixed on earth, that the Gothic types seem to be made over again to special beauties of the master's own invention. The elect and elders indeed, being come to earth, behave with appropriate interest in its attitudes. Galicia is a country of granite, and granite is a fine substance for restraint in carving. One of the attractive qualities of these figures in the Pórtico is that they are less weighted with drapery than much Gothic sculpture, and great interest and attention has been concentrated on actual form and gesture. The arrangement of the feet and draperies of the four and twenty elders seated round the throne in a rainbow arch shows this excellence, but it was for the central shaft above which the figure of the Apostle is seated that the master of the Gloria reserved a precious piece of marble and his utmost virtuosity. The Tree of Jesse is so often a clumsy and artificial genealogical ascent with beauties of detail rather than design. But there is no inch of this shaft which is not lovely and manipulated with obvious delight, from David and Solomon among the leaves to Our Lady emerging from their shade in perpetual innocence and grace.

Something Eastern, suggesting ivories, clings to this tiny shaft, coming, no doubt, by way of Byzantine influence, but also by intention and freshness of design. The figures seated cross-legged in the boughs are accommodated within the tree to perfection, the Oriental posture overcoming the difficulty which confronts august personages whose dignity is to be perpetuated for ever, seated within the branches of a tree. Folds of drapery drawn over the feet, leaves intertwined with the grace of heads bent over musical instruments up to the happy consummation of the Trinity in the capital, make this one of the most delicate miniatures in sculpture.

Even in the dimmest cathedral there is a moment for the obscurest figure, a moment when the sinking or rising light gives animation to an uplifted hand or a deep devotion. And it is when the great west doors in front of the Porch of Glory are opened in the evening that one sees how the vestibule really *is* the Pórtico to the cathedral. Instead of standing against the inside of a door and viewing the sculptured arches as a façade, one recovers the purpose of the canopied dome and the beauty of the figures on the *inside* of the columns. The position of the porch at the head of a long flight of steps brings it high on the cathedral front, and the level sun shines straight in at sundown. The faded colour which covers the figures and draperies deepens and lives. Our Lord sits in glory among His beautiful company, and Santiago the Apostle welcomes the pilgrim. The gifts of the glorified differ in degree. Among the honourable and beautiful company in the Porch of Glory some were saints, some prophets, some evangelists. And the hour of sundown, when every figure there is animated and glowing with the serene purpose of the master, is the hour when Maestro Mateo is himself most visible, kneeling humbly at the base of the arch. For though to some He gave gifts of prophecy and teaching, to others also He gave gifts of skill.

THE ENGLISH CLOCK

Now and again, as one wanders in a foreign country, one is pleasurably confronted by an unexpected 'stray' from one's own. An Anglo-Saxon manuscript in a hill monastery; the embroidery given by an English queen to a church; an English alabaster carving in a treasury; an English clock!

One finds the grandfather clock constantly on the old trade routes by sea. There are two Sheraton clocks in Santa Sofia in Constantinople. There is another in Malaga Cathedral. There was once a great trade in English clocks in Galicia —with its memories of Sir John Moore and Wellington's army of occupation—but now all the clocks are of Swiss manufacture. It was the old clockmaker of Santiago of Compostela indeed who suggested my theme. For in this most Spanish and extraordinary of towns so few English people travel that we are easily noticeable, and the Spaniard, in spite of his taciturnity and gravity, is a simple and unsophisticated person in the main. So as we passed his shop on our way to the café in the afternoon our old clockmaker came out and invited us into his workshop. He had something to show us, something which puzzled him. Would we explain it? He had bought an English clock at a sale some years ago, and had set all the works in order, so that every part worked. The hours and quarters chimed as all the English clocks he had ever seen did chime. The works were very good but not engraved as he had seen in other clocks; very simple, in fact. But there were many things on the dial-plate besides the hours of the day. The actual clock was at his house, but he had made a drawing of the face so that he might ask the señores to explain a matter which was too difficult for him. Here was the drawing.

There were two half-circular dials with numbers such as he had seen on a *calendario perpetuo*. There was a horned moon whose horn pointed to the numbers as the dial revolved. There were two disks, one of which opened gradually and one could see the full moon. In the other was a sailing ship which rocked on a blue sea. He had made all these work, but there was one other thing which was beyond him. Would the señores explain the English words? They were important, evidently, for they were large. Perhaps the señores would explain what they were doing on the clock face:

High Water at Falmouth.

He had looked up 'high water' in the dictionary and found that it meant *marea alta*; but what was Falmouth, and why on the clock? It wasn't the maker's name, for that was elsewhere, and then there was 'high water'! How could one bridge that dilemma? It was such a long way off, and such a different world which suddenly realized itself before us. Such a long way even from the present Falmouth to the old port, where sailing ships put in before proceeding to their home port, 'Falmouth for orders'. Before Liverpool docks, when Bristol was a great port and high water at Falmouth was important enough to be marked on a clock. The old watchmaker waited politely. No! he had never been out of Santiago— had never seen the sea therefore. How could we explain about moons and tides and orders for sailing. 'A great English seaport?' 'Yes?' We stuck. 'Ships sailed at high water.' 'Yes, *marea alta*, certainly; it was there on the clock!' Alas! it was one of those dilemmas with which missionaries are faced, and we had not the vocation or perseverance of such pioneers. We diverted his attention to some antique Spanish ear-rings. The old man was gravely courteous and covered our exit with civilities. He evidently regretted having placed us in an awkward situation before spectators, for he was certain *we didn't know*.

Chapter Twenty

GUADALUPE

One travels to the Royal Monastery of Guadalupe over hills so empty that even at midday one has the sensation of being up early in the morning before anyone else is about; and through heaths as solitary as those of Jura and Skye. Startled animals shy at travellers. Sheep run trotting far from the road. Shepherds with conical velvet hats push through the cistus bushes to look their hardest at a stranger, and one remembers the rhyme of the corn-lands of the north. 'Already the shepherds are leaving Estremadura. Already they are forsaking their own lands so sad and dark.' Yet it is November and the sun is like a warm June day in England, and as one approaches the monastery the Sierras are cultivated to their summits. Olive gardens and eucalyptus plantations and orchards make a good home-coming from the bare Sierras with their cistus heaths and flocks of running sheep. Above the sobriety of the olive gardens are hill tops of flame where the chestnuts are giving their gold to the sun. For the first settlers in the monastery were of the agricultural order of the Jeronimites, who, by the patronage of royal persons and the possession of an image of the Virgin given by Gregory the Great to San Leandro, hidden in times of difficulty, and miraculously discovered by a shepherd, became rich and powerful, the monastery having in its great days a community of three hundred monks, a royal palace, a hospice for noble guests, an infirmary for pilgrims, and being as a matter of fact a small town full of arts and crafts and industry and schools. The illuminators and silversmiths of Guadalupe were especially famous, and the sumptuous grilles which remain in the church suggest of themselves the size of the monastery forges. The catalogue of the gifts of silver and precious stones and metals reads like the building of Solomon's temple. Queens embroidered robes for the small black image which is the centre of the cult, and every famous person in Spanish history sooner or later rode up the rocky road to the monastery to give homage to the Virgin of Guadalupe. Columbus offered prayers to her for nine days and vowed to call an island by her name. Cortés, being bitten by a scorpion and yet being delivered from death, had an emerald case made by Indians for its body and came to Guadalupe to present it to the Virgin. The explorers and conquerors of the New World carried her image and worship thither—to Peru, to Mexico, to La Plata and Cuzco— and it was in the monastery which holds her image that there took place this year (1928), on a day set apart in Spain, as among the Jews, to remember 'the pit whence they were digged', 'The Day of the Race' (the day, in fact, upon which Columbus discovered America), a solemn coronation of the tiny image by the King and the Cardinal Primate of Spain.

For the crown, an ornate and sumptuous jewel with a wide halo, jewels and gifts had been sent from all over the New World, and the 'Day of the Race' saw the consummation of something so much more Spanish than Spain itself, something indeed so much of race and racial expression, that it seems better to let a Spaniard speak than to offer an English comment. I quote from an article written in the *Estampa* by 'José Polo Benito, decano de la Catedral de Toledo': 'As the rays of the sun declined, the ancient stones on the monastery façade seemed fringed with gold. The sculptured figures in the gargoyles, the friezes, the capitals appeared to stir with the breath of life. In the wide circuit of the Plaza—market and forum, with the beautiful reminder of the atria of the great church above it—stirred and swayed the vast multitude of people. How many were there? Whence had they come? For only answer there are the words of Scripture, "Thy sons shall come from far, thy daughters from the ends of the earth. . . ."

'Mass being finished the Cardinal took his crozier and advanced to the first step of the staircase. His voice, tremulous, full of feeling, fell on the hearts of the people slowly and with solemnity.

' "The Virgin of Guadalupe", he said, "is our Mother! The Virgin of Guadalupe is our Queen! Sons of Spain, do you wish the Virgin of Guadalupe as your Mother and your Queen?"

'Unanimous, full, clamorous, the affirmation resounded, ringing the echoes of the valleys and mountains. He then continued:

' "Interpreting the wish and spirit of our King, I have now to tell you that he is at this moment about to place his royal sceptre at the feet of the Virgin in submission to her as one

day to Jesus Christ the Kingdom of Spain. For our King is
the son of the Queen of Heaven, the Virgin of Guadalupe!
Long live our Catholic Monarch! . . ."

'It is twelve o'clock on this day—the "Day of the Race"!
The Virgin who inspired explorers and colonizers sits on her
throne. On either side are King and Cardinal and behind
them the most genuine representatives of the nation. Already
there lies at its feet the royal sceptre. The august hands now
take the jewel made from offerings of gratitude and with it
adorn the heavenly forehead of Our Lady. It is twelve o'clock
of this day, the "Day of the Race".

'So, on this day and hour, Spain and Heaven have been
joined in the maternal kiss of my Virgin of Guadalupe.'

'Yes, the Gothic is very fine, of course', said a Spanish
artist in the sacristy. 'But it is no longer our taste. We are no
longer so spiritual as that. It is the Baroque which we admire
now. Baroque is the real expression of our more modern
and material religion.'

One is never sure in Spain whether the next moment one
may not be taking part in a picture by Velasquez. Our
arrival at the monastery preceded by a few hours that of the
three Infantes who were spending the night in the hostel.
Next morning, on entering the church, High Mass was being
sung. The three sons of the King knelt at praying chairs with
red silk cushions before them like Philip IV in Velasquez's
picture. Groups of candles in heavy silver candlesticks
lighted each step to the altar. The officers of the suite, their
spurred heels clicking as they moved backwards and forwards, served the mass. High over the altar the Virgin's
crown shone and faded as the light moved. The rich mantle
embroidered and jewelled by Queen Isabella of Portugal

made a discreet enrichment of colour beneath the crown. The tiny brown face of the image looked astonished and helpless.

In the museum are the few remaining riches of the monastery, once so wealthy that silver and gold vessels were melted down to supply the cost of wars or the extermination of heretics without much apparent depreciation of its store. The beautiful panels of blue enamel set on a casket by one of the friars were originally part of a throne of the Virgin whose silver was melted to defray the cost of the battle of Aljubarrota, as was the great *retablo* of silver in the church, and much disappeared to be remodelled and reset in yet costlier form in the monastery workshops. Works of art must have gone from this place in hundreds. One of the enormous illuminated choral books which is shown of the eighty-six which remain is a superb achievement, worthy of a place on the *facistol* in the choir, the largest and surely the finest choir desk of beaten bronze in Spain. The pearl-embroidered cloak of the Virgin made by the jewellers of the monastery in its very quietness and stillness of colour is like a breath from some triumphant age of art. There are gifts of kings still remaining. Mary Tudor presented an altar frontal. The triptych of the Flemish school given by the Catholic Kings lives in beauty long after the donors. The altar frontal of Henry II is of Gothic sweetness and grace. The frontal of 'La Pasión', a series of pictures of the Passion in work of applied silk and velvet, I have never seen equalled in any museum, save an English cope of the twelfth century in the museum of Madrid. But the tale of the treasures of Guadalupe and the Virgin's jewels is now only a tale to be read in an archive. In the sacristy of the church is a succession of pictures by Zurbarán which, since they were spared by the French, suggests the obscurity of his reputation in the days of Napoleon. The occasional paintings by Zurbarán scattered through European galleries give only a hint of this grave serene master. Seen in sequence, as at Guadalupe, these seemly pictures of the monastic life of his own Order, suffused with a sincerity of feeling which recalls Masaccio and painted with such fine mastery of colour, place Zurbarán very high among Spanish painters. The ideal painter of grave persons and gestures, he makes an extended arm in a monk's habit as eloquent as a Raphael. These woollen draperies of monks speak like persons. The attractive qualities of the Spaniard, sobriety and sincerity, are wonderfully set forth by Zurbarán—not without a certain agreeable dryness. When the sequestration of the monasteries occurred in Spain, the French Catholic soldiers had left little for the Spanish government.

Outside, the convent, which, once half fortified castle, half monastery, crowns the hill of Guadalupe, the little town walks on stilts up a steep rocky road which no wheeled vehicle ever attempts. One can walk dry under the arcades on which it is planted the whole length of the town. The middle of the street, sloping to gutters, has as many nimble little black pigs scampering here and there, like puppies, as the dogs will allow. The slipping and scuffling of hoofs goes on all day, and the old road which leads up from the valley must be little changed since Isabella, Columbus, and half a hundred kings rode up it to the shrine of the Virgin of Guadalupe either to offer or to take, or since Richard Ford clattered up the inconvenient stony way to look at the then ruinous convent and to meditate on the enormities committed by French Catholics upon the precious things of their own faith. To-day, the monastery is in the hands of Fran-

ciscan monks who keep a free school for boys and a hostel
for travellers, and new State roads curve in and out of the
valleys with many dangerous zigzags. But the plaza below
the church steps, with its round fountain at which women
gather for water, and asses and cows and horses come to
drink, has an ancient and chattering animation which lays
asleep the sensation which goes with one all the time
through modern Spain, that one is seeing the last of things.

Chapter Twenty-one

TRUJILLO

'THE RELIQUARY OF HISTORY'

As one drives along the Cáceres road across a plain full of light and as wide as the sea, where strange spurred mountains rise like islands in the glimmer, where feathered clouds float like medusae in transparent waters, and the distant Sierras de Gredos purify the horizon with snow, to discover the dead forsaken end of Trujillo rising on its hill of granite is like the sudden lighting upon some ancient acropolis, some remote dead city in the sunlight, the abandoned temples of a vanished people, 'the reliquary of a race'.

At first sight the towers and walls seem but a more laboured placing together of the rocks which cover the plain. The Arab towers, squat in ruin, running round the circumference of the hill, have scarcely more importance than the enormous boulders which cover its slope. Yet never was town built with so definite an ambition as this cradle of Conquistadores. Back from victory, with a new continent at their feet, the dividing of lands in their native province, and the devising of palaces suitable for the great, the legitimizing of the illegitimate, became their preoccupation. Throughout the upper part of the town—the ancient *villa*—the splendid Renaissance palaces built by the returned Conquerors show the importance of the town after the Conquests. The towers of granite rise in lordly dilapidation above the Plaza Mayor, where once the tale of notable families was enough to people Spain with hidalgos and heroes. The house of Francisco Pizarro, the conqueror of Peru, has barely enough wall left to carry his belated coat of arms, and only the shell of the castle of the Altamiranos traces the outline of a medieval power.

The town, of course, placed as it is in the centre of the plain, the hub of diverging roads, had a strategic importance long before the conquest of Peru and the Indies. Arab and Roman impressions still are there, but its history began for Spain with the Conquistadores. Its privileges were enormous, each king adding one more, until the affairs of 'Montagues and Capulets' between the powerful ruling families brought about another settlement by Charles V with order and a municipal government. The palaces, built to impress, are some of them gigantic. The Plateresque corner window and detail of doorways have a delightful effect in the narrow uphill streets where, were it not for this architectural device, they would present a high cliff to the eye from the footways. Some—that of the seignorial house known as the 'House of the Staircase'—are beautiful, some dignified, some—that of the Pizarros with a coat of arms such as a savage might choose, of Indians led in chains and Atahualpa carrying his chest of treasure—portentous. Relics of medieval powers linger in some—a thick heavy chain hung within the great doorway of the house 'Orellanas-Chavis' stood for the right of asylum granted to its lords. The name 'Merced' on a street corner recalls the history of the house of Franciscans which sheltered the Molière-like poet-monk 'Tirso de Molina', and whose work was the raising of money for the redemption of Christian slaves from the Moorish galleys.

Only one church has anything of much value within it, but that of Santa María la Mayor has so beautiful a painted *retablo* in the early Flemish style that a painter might well turn aside to meditate. Either the convents and churches were emptied by the French or the devotion of the Conquistadores went to Guadalupe.

Trujillo seems a tiny place, as it stands isolated in the plain, for so much to have resulted there. It must now, one thinks, be the largest town in Spain unvisited by any railway. The roads, setting off in every direction from the hill, or reaching it from circular horizons, are still of first importance, since every one must come in and out by them, and the variety of travellers is as great as the measure of Spain. On this day of our visit the town has attained a superlative cleanliness. Streets are being washed. Man, woman, and child is sweeping and scouring. The King is driving over the plain to-morrow to visit the town of the Conquistadores, and as the small girl from out of her attendant clouds of dust explained to me, 'His Majesty comes to-morrow, so we are doing a little cleaning'.

Along the Cáceres road, stone dykes separate pasture from

pasture (with the wide grass margins for travelling flocks), and if it were not for this abundant sun which even in mid-November fills a cloudless canopy with a white glare, the immediate landscape brings a reminder of Yorkshire or Cumberland fells. The sheep feeding, some white, some black, bring the dowry of Catherine of Lancaster to the recollection—'so many white sheep', the profitable source of England's wealth in her day.

The King's way lay through a modest suburb of the town, and here a little arch of palm leaves spanned the road—(not quite high enough to clear the King's carriage, for some of the greenery lay on its roof when he drove to the Plaza). All was running in and out and shaking of gay mantones of silk from their folds to hang as flags above the roads. The boys arranged them with long poles. The girls chattered and laughed; the Guardia Civil admired and suggested. Perhaps the King missed most of the fun when he arrived to find it all ready, but the girls and boys would hardly have had it otherwise.

Now he is escorted to see the new gift to the town—the statue of Francisco Pizarro, Conquistador of Peru, sculptured by the sculptor Rumsey and cast in bronze in Paris. It is a romantic conception and well placed in the Plaza beneath the steps of the Plateresque church of San Martín. The Conquistador rides on his horse, his lance in rest, the feathers on his helmet flying—a Mambrino of conquerors. The accomplishment of the group is not equal to its conception, unfortunately, but it has the merits as a sculptured heroic group of ambition, effort, and effect.

From above, the medieval *villa* of dark granite, rusty with lichen and clustered against the plain like a group of watchmen, shows all the suspicions and dangers of its period. The towers stand close, the roofs press in upon them. One can hardly suspect other footways than galleries for men-at-arms between them. Close, secretive, with Moorish signs in the towers, the streets climb between high walls to the Arab citadel (not in itself remarkable save for its dominance of so superb a panorama and its own area), past a square ancient bathing-pool, said to be of Arab origin, to the broken house of Pizarro, his coat of arms hanging to a ruinous wall, his conquest an episode in history. An old woman climbs the street laboriously. Pushing open the gate beneath the *escudo* of Pizarro the Conqueror, she throws corn to her fowls. A cat runs after her, peering beneath the shut gate. Footsteps ring on a stone floor behind the gate of the convent at our back. Someone inside turns a key with a loud noise. Then the footsteps retreat again to some buried and far-away interior. The old woman comes out to the street again. She looks round at the roofless houses, the ruined walls, and up at the *escudo* of Pizarro. 'Es muy histórica, pero falta mucho,' she sighs, 'falta mucho.' (It is very historical but there is a great deal lacking.) A little light twinkles at dusk in the highest point of the citadel where the Virgin of Victory has a chapel. Of the towers looking down on the wide Plaza one is given over to the meditations of nuns, others are silent and empty. Clustered in a grave group against the landscape, their suspicions and silences as much for defence from within as from without, dovecotes, nunneries, bell-towers, they wait their dissolution in the background of the Plaza where rides the new statue of Francisco Pizarro, Conquistador, the feathers of his helmet flying airily against the stars, his lance couched and tilting at the unattainable Pleiades.

Chapter Twenty-two

CÁCERES

Whereas in Trujillo all the upper medieval town is broken and abandoned and its quiet that of the graveyard, the palaces of Cáceres are still occupied by families of repute, and the quiet within its steep, involved, and cobbled streets is that of the absence of traffic. Since no wheeled vehicles venture there, when the streets are often interrupted by steps and the stately old palaces stand aloof remembering their history, all the business and chatter of the newer town circles the hill beneath them—like a stream. The townspeople climb the hill for church and municipal affairs.

It is a long time since I wandered in the Appian Way and sighed over the tomb of Cecilia Metella. Suddenly Rome seems a short time ago and its distance bridged by a human

[169]

link, for the town camp of Cáceres was built by the Roman, Caecilius Metellus—alas! they never thought very much of him.

In waterless Cáceres water plays an important part. The life of the streets owes much in colour to the water-carriers. Its fountains are thronged with women and girls, who carry a very tall and graceful classic pitcher upon their heads, supporting it upon a circular padded wad of gay colours from which hangs a pendant behind. Processions of women walk with the easy dignified carriage of those who bear weights on their heads, climbing the steep streets with a slow dignity as if performing some ritual of the highway, their beautiful jars appearing like the strange head-dress of some slow rhythmic dance or rite.

But the strangest relic in Cáceres is in the site of the old Moorish Alcázar and a legacy of the ancient Arabian wisdom in water. The underground cisterns of Yeri Batán in Constantinople have a smaller counterpart in Cáceres. But whereas those of Constantine are like a vast Byzantine cathedral flooded with water, with Byzantine capitals to the pillars, between which one glides in a light boat, those of Cáceres are supported on heavy horseshoe arches and are only the size of a considerable swimming-bath. In time of siege and drought this city on the hill in the centre of a wild heath reaching to mountain barriers must have blessed the Arabian knowledge and skill in storing cool water.

From the window of the house of the Veletas one looks over the country. The walls are below. The two strange Moorish defence towers are on either side, remains of smaller towers show broken edges. The fortified palace of the Moorish Emir, with its cisterns of water, seemed impregnable in its position. The men of Babel were not alone in history in their desire to build a tower to make them as gods. The chastisement of pride and presumption was measured out in Cáceres. San Gimignano of the beautiful towers suffered no more drastic curtailment of the arrogance of its nobles than did Cáceres under the order of Isabella the Catholic. 'All towers to be cut down to the level of the roofs of the houses, except that of the family of Captain Diego Cáceres Ovando, for services to the Catholic Kings in the battle of Toro', must have been a formidable object-lesson in the fifteenth century. That is why one looks upward in the street and sees a gallery on corbels fit for a castle high on the wall of a house, and only by going to the side of the street one sees the roof cutting short what was evidently the base of a strong and high tower. Towers built later and after Isabella's death are not so threatening nor so arrogant. From the plain there is a fine barbed crest of them running along the ridge of the town.

Roman foundations, unmistakable as Roman rectitude, carry the Roman working plan. The gate of Santo Cristo, serviceable and robust, is pure Roman. Inscriptions are built into the walls of houses, and above the tower of the clock in the market-place stands the antique Roman statue of Ceres, colossal, august.

The Arabian remains are more scattered. The towers of the old Alcázar and the Moorish wall and tower upon the Roman foundations raise a miniature Alhambra on the hill of Cáceres, and Moorish brickwork is seen here and there in the house fronts and their culture in the irrigation of the orchards and gardens. But the lasting imprint of the town is that of the Conquistadores and medieval nobles, whose mutilated towers endure in the clear dry air of the plain.

The cleanliness of Cáceres is purchased by much labour.

The cobbles are brushed energetically by the women with short besoms of green broom, and the water carried from steep distances. One never ceases wondering what that exile who built a palace in Cáceres thought of Spain when he had crossed the Atlantic. Perhaps the prospect of recrossing the sea was worse than the thought of staying. Perhaps travel enlarged his mind—or perhaps simply he was never allowed to go back. The 'sun in his splendour' marks the house assigned to this child of the sun—a grim little plaza contains the palace—a circumscribed life for an emperor, one thinks, with the rainbow fading on the Andes.

San Salvador de Val-de-Dios

Rock Tomb of King Pelayo, Covadonga

Chapter Twenty-three

MÉRIDA

ROMA AETERNA

The Romans have won Mérida for good. True, every one who ever left an imprint on the Spanish race has passed through the once magnificent capital of Lusitania, but of Visigoth and Moor hardly any traces remain, of the Renaissance nothing, of the Templars a 'mountain of ruins'. So that one now leaves Spain, becoming no longer a traveller in the Iberian Peninsula, but in ancient Rome, treading the quiet paths of the archaeologist, pensive with other memories, of Palatine and Pincian Hills, of Capitol and Forum, of the roomy and sovereign empires of Augustus, Trajan, and Hadrian. I have my own strong conviction that the Spaniard more than any other Latin nation continues the features and ideal of the Roman, but the familiar quiet of the grass-grown and sunny Circus, the Stadium, the theatre, that elaborate architectural housing for the human voice, the heavy solemnity of the aqueduct, these dominations of an empire whose emperors were gods belong to an older world than Spain. Perhaps the very decay and unimportance of Mérida in the time of Spain's great building epoch after the Reconquest saved the Roman monuments from being further despoiled. No considerable palace seems to have been erected on the spot. Visigoth and Moor had taken all they wanted of column and moulding. The earth lay lightly on Eternal Rome. Beside the ruins, at which the learned are now busy, the town lies like an Arab town, unable to open out into views, its chimneyless house roofs lying close and almost overlapping, one narrow street disclosing nothing until one turns into the next, its whitewashed house fronts striking an Oriental dazzle to the eyes. How relentless is the Roman bridge which led to the splendours of Mérida! Its half-mile of narrow, undeviating level lies over the Guadiana like an ordeal by sunlight. Before one has gone half-way one has the feeling of being unable to turn back. One must go on, caught in the forced march across, or die in the returning. Once in that formidable narrow alley, horses, oxen, carts, donkeys, as men, are all under the lash of necessity. Fortitude wavers. One is no longer an individual. Legions march with one to an imperial command—I want more room.

More kindly is the stride of the aqueduct over my head. The flickering of olives beneath it, the passing of wings about it, do not abash the gravity of its antiquity. Its ruin is portentous but beneficent, its iron-grey piers being a kind of St. Kilda of the beanfields, its use solved by the migratory storks.

'Ah! you should have been here earlier when the storks were here. Then they ("los milagros" is the country name) were a much better sight. Every one of the miracles has its population of storks. Now it is *very* solitary and the nests have been ruined by bad weather and wind. But when they begin to come, on the day of San Blas, it becomes very animated. Hundreds of storks come here, all the miracles have their nests. It is a *población* of storks.' So our ploughman told us, as proud of the storks as of the miracles and not very sure that they were not somehow indissolubly connected.

'Ay . . . ye, Amorita! Otra vez!' He turns his mules and the 'Beloved' staggers 'once more' to the hard furrows.

What a beautiful white house of colonnaded marble this imperial race built here for its intellectual diversion! One is so accustomed to see sculptured marble figures like that of the goddess Ceres in the orderly twilight of museums, that one blinks in the bright sun to see gods and warriors, garlands and oxen, dancers and flowers and all the prodigality of marble art, set in position again in the marble proscenium. The reconstruction is being done with great discretion and taste. One wing of the proscenium is now almost complete —a lordly pleasure-house, a stage strangely permanent for the human drama which was vocal there as a wind that passes and echoes. On one side are the lovely columns of the vestibule; on the other, in a back street behind the theatre, is the humble Christian basilica of the early Roman settlers, a tiny dissenting chapel of brick, the feet of saints and confessors still showing in the red glazed Pompeian decoration of its interior, the anagram of Christus in the mosaic pavement of its atrium. There were palaces of Visigoths and the Alcázar of Moorish rulers—Castle of Templars and Knights of Santiago—but one great edifice accommodated many changes. So that the mighty stones of El Conventual may have been placed in position many times—only the Visigothic ornament is unmistakable, and the cistern of waters in the ruined Alcázar carries their tradition. Columns worked and laboured like ivories, palm-trees—alder leaves—birds in flocks—plaited rope—Solomonic pillar, such museum remnants show the passing of this race of fine architects through ancient Lusitania. I said that the Romans won Mérida, but the town has for its patron saint a young girl-martyr, Santa Eulalia (Olalla), whom the Romans roasted in an oven. From as early as the fourth century comes the Visigothic inscription found near her church.

'May this house be under thy peaceful rule, O martyr Eulalia, so that the enemy, knowing of thy protection, may be confounded, and that this house and its inhabitants may flourish beneath thy patronage. Amen.'

They have made a sort of amende to Santa Eulalia by reconstructing a portico of an old temple dedicated to Mars by 'Vetilla, wife of Paculo' upon the traditional site of her martyrdom. Whatever primitive church bore her name, the present one is of an unusual and grand form of Romanesque, a basilica of lofty halls, echoing something pagan, something of majesty. A strange and imposing interior—an architectural development of Romanesque, as unusual as impressive.

I leave the theatre with its stone hall. Up on an eminence where the temple of Mithras and Serapis stood is the Plaza de Toros—the great circular Colosseum of Spain—so much too large for the size of the town. It too is Roman in scale. I eat a dish of lamb's liver stewed with the peel of fresh oranges for lunch—I feel sure that Lucian ate it long ago.

Chapter Twenty-four

OVIEDO AND THE ASTURIAN CHURCHES

THE BOOK OF CHRONICLES

When the meticulous mind of Philip II thought out the plan of sending Ambrosio Morales to make a chronicle of the 'relics, tombs of royal personages, and libraries' in all the churches and monasteries in the north of Spain, he arranged, though without intention, a gentler picture of the priest of his time than its fiery and dominant history has often allowed. Ambrosio Morales, devout, scrupulous, and diligent, took his commission and his exactitude, and journeyed from convent to convent in the year 1572. He was to tabulate relics and books; to see in what condition these were kept, and especially to record the reverence paid to the tombs of the kings and whether, money having been left to the monasteries for the purpose of masses being sung, these were duly and properly carried out. For a record one needs a starting-point, and that of Morales was duly decided by the King.

'He [Philip II] also related how he had enquired much of the head of San Lorenzo which he had heard was kept in a monastery in Galicia, without stating where. With this I began to carry out my commission in Valladolid.'

King Philip thus ensuring a genuine search, the devout and kindly Morales sets out, with few suspicions and several private curiosities of his own, one of which was to discover, as he went about, 'the true value of the ancient maravedi of Castile'.

His records are candid and naïve. He relates how in such and such a monastery he could not see the relics, 'the abbot [wisely, it may be] not being at home'. Sometimes relics of holy saints are displayed with organ music and much pomp. Again, he tells how the books in a certain library have most of them been sold for old vellum. He admonishes the monks in certain convents for their treatment of their books. For San Fructuoso, the Visigothic saint of the Bierzo, he pleads with indignant eloquence. 'These books', he admonishes the abbot of San Pedro de Montes, 'ought to be better kept and reverenced. They ought, in fact, to be treated as holy relics of the saint. From them he drew the life of his spirit. From them he took comfort and they were his loyal companions. Surely then they were closer to the *real* saint than such things as sandals and clothing, and more deserving to be treated therefore with respect and duly preserved.' Of San Benito, in Valladolid, he writes that it was founded by the Gothic King Chindasvinto, who is there interred. The tomb of this

Arian king is at one side of the church under a canopy with a grille before it. 'They regard him as a saint in that country, and the monastery has a history divided into nine "lessons", as if for reading at matins, and it is a pity to see how fictitious and fabulous it is. I have already said to those fathers how unworthy it is of their great piety and prudence to keep that history and in such a manner.'

Not to believe everything he is told, he goes to the Cámara Santa at Oviedo, and though he writes of his visit to the relics in this manner, 'I am now writing in the church before the grille, and God knows that I am almost beside myself with fear and reverence, and I cannot do more than beseech God to help me to perform that which I alone cannot do'; yet of the Cross of the Angels (which tradition declared to have been wrought by two angels disguised as goldsmiths) he 'believes the front only to have been worked by angels, and if indeed they did the back [which he doubts] then some one else added the inscription, for the letters are of later date'.

He dismisses as spurious the coin taken from the fish's mouth, for the Jews had no coinage, but used the Roman mint, 'Did not our Lord, in asking for a penny, call attention to the image of Caesar upon it?' A date was a lighthouse in research.

He has a dignified manner of treating slanders. He mentions the 'funny story' that Alfonso the Chaste and his wife Berta slept in separate chapels one on each side of the altar to dismiss it in this wise: 'It is a fable, because this church was built after their death, and apart from this the invention is unworthy and improper'. Now and again this chronicle of relics and royal tombs digresses into personal appreciation and zest. His delight in the 'Roman antiquity' at Husillos—a tomb 'which Berruguete thought better than anything in Italy, and worthy to be placed beside the best work in that country'—makes amends to him for the task of censure when prelates borrow books from monasteries and neglect to return them. 'The memorandum says that he will return them in four or five months, and more than a year has passed since he took them, and the three or four last, it appears, were given. In such bad security as this I found everything here.'

Since the 'Sacred Journey' of his commission from the King took him through the Asturias, it is from Ambrosio Morales that one learns how the early churches of the mountains were conditioned and standing in his day, he having a great liking for the Roman and Goth in his ancestry.

THE ASTURIAN CHURCHES

In the Kingdom of the Asturias, where something of Roman but hardly anything of Moorish has left its trace, stand the earliest of all the existing Spanish churches— churches, that is, remaining entire as they were built, and not now incorporated, as in the crypt of Palencia, into other and later buildings. An English traveller visiting these mountain churches of the Spanish-Goths has more than a passing impression of the resemblance of these simple primitive temples to the Saxon churches of the same date still standing in England, and of the similarity of much Celtic decoration to the flat bands of carved ornament, the roundels and enriched slabs and pierced stone which form the decoration of the Asturian churches.

If from the history of the development of the basilica (the emergence of the Christian worship from its secrecy in

Roman houses to its finding for itself a building after the arrangement of such a house), from the liturgical arrangements and usages of the primitive Church everywhere, from the reaction of Roman, Goth, and Moorish styles one on the other, from the trade between East and West and the innovations in building carried by travelling masons and builders, the architecture of the Asturian churches can spread into an important branch of study, there is sufficient on the surface to detain even the unlearned.

It is probable that the customs of the primitive liturgy may explain the architectural 'fixture' of style, since the humble Christian churches were built for a definite purpose alone, the housing of a number of people to hear and celebrate a mystery—the initiate within the church, the uninitiate or catechumens outside. 'Let the building be long [says a third-century canon], with its head to the east, with its vestries on both sides at the east end, and so it will be like a ship.' They must not be grand, for beauty is in God. No portrayal of the Cross or Passion might be made, or sculptured figure in the round. Parts of the service were conducted only after a curtain had been drawn between priest and people. The altar was placed between the seats of bishop and priest and the congregation. Cross and lights were hung above the altar, not placed upon it.

The passage of architectural ideas from country to country made for a synchronization of styles. There came the change from wooden churches (one such still surviving in England at Greenstead in Essex) and wooden-roofed churches, to those of stone, the carving which had been done in wood still leaving ideas for ornament in stone, the jewel-work, brooch, and targe, so much more advanced than other arts, suggesting decorative motives. Dogmas also, at the suppression of Arianism, may have left traces in architectural ornament; the threefold cord twined and plaited, the grouping of churches in threes, the apse with three chapels, may be a perpetual reminder of the now dominant doctrine of the Trinity.

'Business' of the church was kept distinct from the celebration of the mystery, the porch (as at Bradford-on-Avon) being an important place in which the first part of the marriage service, of baptism, and such rites as the churching of women were celebrated. It was a shelter for catechumens and unbaptized, who might watch the mystery from afar. This may explain the smallness of the church proper. Only the initiate might enter. Burial also took place in the porch.

In the church of San Salvador de Val de Dios, near Villaviciosa, is a three-roomed porch above whose lintel on the inner side, the door into the church proper, is this inscription:

'*May this be called the church of the Saviour. To Him we dedicate all benefices and sanctuaries which we build here. Afar let him be from here who presumptuously seeks to break these vows. May he be deprived, O Christ, of Thy light. May the earth cover him alive. May his offspring have their place with the beggar and the leper.*'

Here is the same prohibition to the unregenerate from the church proper and the explanation of the porch, while in the vaulted openings on either side was the place for burial, which was prohibited within the church. 'One of my friends is buried there', said a novice. 'Those who have examined, even in the most cursory manner, the internal arrangements of our ancient churches' (*i.e.* English), writes Bloxam, 'cannot have failed to notice that many of them contain, either over the porch or over the vestry . . . a loft or habitable chamber, of which no record or even tradition remains as to the use or purpose for which it was constructed.' In such rooms apparently anchorites were secluded, some even being built for the purpose and the door walled up after the solemn entrance of the recluse—access afterwards being only through the window. In rudimentary monastic foundations they were used as sleeping places for the religious. So, above the three-roomed porch of San Salvador de Val de Dios, are three apartments reached by a flight of stone steps in which the priests slept, and a hidden room above the altar at the east end is reached only by a ladder set to the window. A similar hidden room is found in the same position in the church of St. Julian of the Meadows in Oviedo, but whether for recluse or church treasure no record remains.

Ritual also explains the trace of the Eikonostasis in these early churches. In England 'the chancel was separated from the body of the church by a curtain or veil extending across the chancel arch (*extenso velo inter eos et populum*)'.

'In all countries of the Eastern Orthodox church,' writes Dr. Pullan, 'part of the service is hidden from the worshippers because it is conducted behind the picture-screen (Eikonostasis) in front of the altar. This is simply an Eastern development of the screen of columns and curtains which in more primitive times stood in front of the altar.' So in the church of Santa Cristina de Lena, at the head of two divided stairs of five steps each, stands a row of marble columns upholding a beautiful pierced screen of stone, the altar with its carved slab standing in the middle of the tribune which the Eikonostasis divides from the church. Such screens of columns stand also in other early churches of Spain like San Miguel de Escalada.

'In the year A.D. 676 [about the date of the Venerable Bede] Benedict Biscop built the church of the monastery of Monkwearmouth, having sent for masons from Gaul to construct it of stone after the Roman manner', and so we read that 'In their day these churches [Asturian] were very famous as the first churches built without wood'. But just as in Monkwearmouth the stone ornament was like a wooden decoration in stone, so much of the carving in the Asturian churches reminds one of the wood carving of Scandinavia, old ironing-boards, and domestic utensils, carved brackets, and borders, with resemblances here and there to Runic patterns and knots.

Ideas of vaulted stone roofing were travelling from place to place. East and West were reacting on one another as churchmen and workmen travelled here and there. The Asturian churches themselves are the fruit of the Spanish-Gothic line of kings and their desire to consolidate their religion with their kingdom. For the conquest of extermination which the last Moorish invasion carried through the Peninsula left no Christian building standing in its path, and what was rebuilt on earlier and ruined foundations shows the imprint of Oriental ideas.

But in the Asturias, regained and kept through this invasion by the Spanish-Goths, these early churches were built apart from the ideas of the conquerors, following, it is reasonable to suppose, a traditional style of architecture such as had been used by the earlier Goths from Roman style familiar in the country itself, avoiding purposely any hint of the Moorish enemy, but showing, nevertheless, such details of Oriental ornament as suggests a reflection of the East, whether by way of ivories, glass, or textiles, or by new ideas travelling thither by way of Lombard masons and carvers who worked on the Mediterranean coast. (The cave of Covadonga holds a tiny church, laboriously made to contain within itself every ornamental motive which the architect could find in these early and Visigothic churches of Spain. Brought all together in this way the impression is of a completely Oriental interior.)

The early Gothic kings in Spain built with some splendour when at last they practised the arts. 'King Sisebut built in Toledo the church of St. Leocadia *with much beautiful work.*' The votive crowns in Madrid and the Louvre carry the name of Resceswindus, and 'San Isidoro relates of this very Catholic prince, that he adorned with many gifts of gold and silver, precious stones and rich hangings, the churches and all pertaining to the divine cult', and of the church of San Juan de Baños he says, 'that it has many rich marbles and jaspers of various colours such as the Goths used in their churches' (MORALES).

Whether or no Alfonso the Chaste, who consolidated the small Christian Kingdom recovered by Pelayo, was anxious to establish in his capital of Oviedo something of the state and importance of the Visigothic empire of Leovigild at Toledo, he certainly built there palaces and churches, and is reputed to have 'sent long distances for precious marbles, and workmen fit to carve and adorn'. It was he who built the 'Holy Chamber', enclosed in the Cathedral of Oviedo as a shrine for the relics gathered and guarded by the small Christian state. It is chiefly from outside, from an old grave-yard leading to the cloister of the cathedral, that one can see the resemblance of this high-roofed building rising above a vaulted undercroft with two flat tombs carved in the Visigothic manner to the other high-roofed Asturian churches. With the Cámara Santa there are San Julián of the Meadows,

[185]

San Tirso, San Miguel de Lino, Santa María de Naranco, Santa Cristina de Lena, and across the mountains in Val de Dios is the church of San Salvador, and at Priesca still another.

This group of churches escaped the hammer of Almanzor when those of León were ravaged and the Christian Kingdom thrust back into the Asturias, and have so many characteristics in common that they are taken as the type of native Spanish architecture; architecture, that is, which the Spaniard himself was developing (as, in subject India, the Hindu interpretation will thrust its head above the Mohammedan custom) from his earlier traditions, 'Latin in structure, with echoes of the East, but with additional and local features'.

SANTA MARÍA DE NARANCO

On the green hillside of Naranco looking down on the old Gothic capital of Oviedo, near the site where Ramiro I (842–850) built a palace and royal baths, stand two of the famous early churches of Asturias—San Miguel de Lino and Santa María. When Ambrosio Morales passed by in 1572 he commented in his own manner upon them.

'The rich palaces, so celebrated in our history, which King Ramiro also made here near these two churches, remain on the ground, though only their ruins are standing. Thus it is evident how much more care the king took and commanded to be put into the building of the Temples than of his own house, those enduring with great stability while his house has fallen in ruins.'

'*Ramiro the glorious prince, with Paterna his wife and queen, renewed this little dwelling, decrepit with age*', reads part of the dedication stone of Santa María, and reclining on the slope of its green hill, like a belvedere with the Asturian mountains as its prospect, the little church restored by Ramiro and his wife has never given up the secret of its real origin. For these days it had magnificent ambition and plan—a long apartment like the room of a palace, with open arcaded vestibules at either end, with a stone barrel-vaulted roof, banded tight like the keel of a ship. The weight of opinion goes to suggest that Santa María was not intended for a church, but was part of the palace of Ramiro, converted into an oratory. The wrong orientation of the church has added colour to this belief, but the orientation of early churches was not invariably right; sometimes, as in St. Peter's itself and St. Paul's outside the Walls at Rome, the orientation was changed to meet the difficulties of situation, as in this case it might very well be. But whether palace room or private oratory of the King, since the year A.D. 866 mass has been said without a break in a consecrated church, as undisturbed on this autumn morning as an English Downland sanctuary. As in rural England also, the farmers and labourers are busy at country occupations, and under the robe of Saint Antony, patron of animals, are tucked innumerable celluloid pigs, goats, and calves for his recollection while the people are at work in the fields. At the door, on a levelled platform of earth, six men beat their harvested sheaves with flails. The men stand in a ring, shadowless in the golden light, and the flails rise and fall like a ritual. This also has continued without a break for centuries. Something very noble greets one in this primitive church—the procession of its outside buttresses adding strength to dignity, the interior work (its rope ornament giving the impression of a church which had the devotion of sailors) so careful and beautiful. 'All the ornament is flat, and the beauty of the church is in its fine proportion and line,' concluded Morales, the 'flatness' having a strange quality of low relief as of ivories. This smooth enrichment by carving, the decoration never supplementing or hiding noble proportion or line, but placed only where it would have value to enrich it, shows the tranquil adumbration of a fine architecture of 'place' already native in the Spaniard-Goth. Nowhere does ornament take from the precision and dignity of architectural shape. The stone roof-ribs descending to an exact propriety between each flat wall-arch and filling the spandrel with its carved roundel, the bands of work like the gold borders of robes, the twin-pillars of the wall arcading with their curious spiral formation, the hanging disks, the once open galleries at either end, the hitherto unused construction of the stone vault—all these are amply discussed by the learned architects both of France and Spain. Whether this method of constructing and decorating a church came by way of Lombardy, or by way of northern prisoners of war in the days of Ramiro I; whether the hanging carved roundels (so like the flat country loaves to this day) are like the votive shields hung in Greek temples or the halls of northern warriors, whether the open galleries at either end allowed the congregation to worship from the hillside, are matters which may never be solved completely.

What is it that makes these diminutive churches so impressive, so that they impose, even at first sight, the sense of dignity and solemnity one expects only from a larger building? Santa Cristina de Lena, the solitary 'hermitage' high on its crag above the river, has the impressiveness of its situation among mountains; San Salvador shares the sunny peace of its 'Valley of God'; but San Julián of the Meadows has no setting from which it can borrow. Yet the same importance rises about its old walls, the same quality of sincerity and loftiness about its ancient enduring stone.

Height, perhaps (as in the Saxon churches these buildings for their size are always of great height), simplicity of mass, sincerity of ornament, and great fitness for their original purpose. Bare almost to poverty in these days, they suggest a simple race and fine architects. The trumpet, not the bell, one feels, would sound for this worship. The soldier would be attentive in the worshipper.

SAN SALVADOR DE VAL DE DIOS

' "*Thy great mercy, O Lord, shines in every place and many times saves the sinner. All men confess that Thou givest life to the dead and light in the darkness. Be pleased, already most bountiful in mercy, to pardon and succour this unhappy one, since my soul is wounded and fallen through the mortal sins which I have committed. Shew forth on my behalf Thy pardoning grace, with which Thou liftest the fallen, and help with the same pity with which Thou dost protect and uphold those who are in this world, and workest blessedness to those who dwell in heaven.*"

'Seven bishops consecrated this temple:

RUDICINDO OF DUNSIO	*ARGIMIERO OF LAMEGO*
NAUSTIS OF COIMBRA	*RECAREDO OF LUGO*
SISNANDO OF PADRON	*ELLECANA OF ZARAGOZA*
RANULFO OF ASTORGA	

in the year 931 of the Era' (which is that of 893 of Jesus Christ).

This consecration stone of the church of San Salvador de Val de Dios, the most unchanged of the Visigothic churches in the Asturias, is a long upright slab in the outer wall of the church, protected by a low cloister. If the inscription is indeed of this early date, its simplicity and directness give much of the feeling which the buildings of these primitive sanctuaries convey.

This church, dedicated to the Saviour, lies in the 'Valley of God', in the north of the Asturias, among wide and venerable chestnut trees, full of sun and peace. It is the least changed of all the Asturian churches from its original plan, probably having been saved from additions by the building of an ad-joining abbey and church at a later date, which satisfied the requirements of a large congregation. The cloister which connected the small San Salvador with the abbey until, apparently, some twenty years ago, has been taken away and the simplicity and dignity of this characteristic Asturian church is seen unimpeded. A very high nave—long in pro-portion to its width; at either side a lower aisle, narrow, and of the length of the church, leaving room above for a clere-story of delicate double windows, divided by small balusters beneath twin arches, each pair cut from one stone. Double images of sunlight are cast through these windows upon the expanse of wall over the arcade. The gable of the sanctuary is not so tall as that of the nave. It is flanked, like the nave, by aisles with lean-to roofs, but it juts out slightly beyond them. On either side of this threefold building was built a small chapel—forming the cross-beam of the cross. Only one of these now stands at San Salvador, though the evi-dences of the other remain.

At the west end is a threefold porch, corresponding to the threefold chapels at the east end. The secret rooms above it have already been described. Beyond this porch (or outer church, for it is included in the main outer wall), sinners and the impenitent were refused entrance.

The canonical instruction, 'Let the building be high', has been faithfully observed, though the hidden room above the altar and reached by a ladder makes the sanctuary very low as seen from the interior. No window betrays the existence of the room from within, but that visible on the outer wall of the church is a lovely Mozárabe decoration with slender marble shafts.

The whole building leads the architect Van Pelt to say (*Romanesque and Allied Styles of Spanish Architecture*): 'The church of San Salvador de Val de Dios is suggestive of what might be done in a small village church by the contrast of openings and a plain wall surface'.

At either end of the long high roof of the middle aisle is an upright rough ornament like an oak-leaf, and along the ridge are stone knobs reminding one of the decoration on Etruscan tombs. On one side has been built later a delicate arched cloister with pierced stone windows and pillars of Mozárabe design beautifully worked, the familiar patterns of rope and veined leaves being repeated here with greater skill than in the church itself.

Inside, the great height of the central roof is covered by a barrel vaulting. The space above the sanctuary is bare save for two brackets. From these hung a curtain before the altar was consecrated. One only of the side vestries remains. The two round marble pillars on either side the sanctuary have the flat-veined alder-leaf capital, those in each of the side chapels a Corinthian decoration. The arcades, very low in proportion to the height of the nave, are supported on heavy square pillars of stone, with chamfered edges and square heavy capitals, the capitals and bases being identical and having for ornament two deeply incised lines. There are all the familiar features of the Asturian basilican churches—the

threefold aisles with roofs lifted high—the cross chapels—
the Mozárabe windows with delicate rope ornament and
designs of veined alder-leaves—and the strength and majesty
of the building.

In the lower sides of the pillars nearest the sanctuary are the
grooves for admitting the low carved stone slabs which
separated the presbytery from the congregation.

Seven bishops travelled to this valley in the year 893 to
consecrate this tiny building. Who was the 'sinner' whose
prayer fills the stone of consecration? 'A son of St. Bernard',
say the priests within whose grounds it lies. The leaves of
the apple-trees and the maize rustle about it this evening. If it
were not for the voices of the two hundred seminarists in the
college adjoining, one might see the procession of the seven
bishops approaching through the orchard.

Chapter Twenty-five

COVADONGA

SANCTUARY

Higher even than the trilling of the *grillos*, into the heart of the mountain silences, with Pelayo's waterfall and source of the Deva pouring on in the quiet, with a moon like a silver shield travelling on the hill tops, one is happy if one arrives at Covadonga in an autumn sundown. For then the way up the wooded valleys glows like a shell of the Indian Ocean. The heather knolls are withered to a bright amber. The groves of chestnut trees, venerable as New Forest oaks, shine sombrely between the illumination of gold lines of autumn poplars, and over the balconies and *solanas* (sunrooms) of the Asturian farms hang the cobs of ripe maize strung in wide mats of orange beneath the coral eaves of sunset.

As one enters the valley of sanctuary in the twilight a deep natural amphitheatre seems to raise savage and forbidding walls about one. But daylight discloses the formidable bendings of the declivities (in places so narrow that one cannot imagine any outlet) which produce the rim of circular heights upon which the clouds travel for ever as on a wheel, and where, in the folded and craggy angle of a high grey cliff, lies the cave of refuge which sheltered the Gothic king Pelayo with thirty men and ten women, and from which the recovery of Asturias, and so, in the end, of Spain, from the Muslim was finally accomplished. From beneath it rushes a full cascade of waters which give rise to the river Deva, a stream plunging deep into the valley, which, followed backward, would lead a fugitive to the cave of sanctuary. The cliff, an imposing and formidable height, leans forward with an inclination steep enough to shelter the opening where, within two natural recesses of this lions' den, lie the plain sarcophagi of Pelayo the Visigoth and Alfonso the First, the consolidator of Pelayo's kingdom and the founder of the church and monastery below the cave. A long stone flight of steps leads to the chapel of the cave, 'La gruta', up which the peasant women climb on their knees. From below, the sound of prayer and singing issuing from the cave, above the sound of the waters rushing from beneath the feet of the worshippers, as it has done for 800 years, makes this 'place of worship' one of the most astonishing in western Europe.

The history of Pelayo,[1] the William Wallace of Spain, is less in the dim ages of epic than that of many other heroes who 'took to the heather'. From Arabian as well as Christian sources the tale in its essentials gives the freedom of Spain to

[1] Pelayo, a Gothic king elected after the death of Roderick, whose victory over the Moors at Covadonga (A.D. 718) began the Christian reconquest of Spain. Died 737.

the sword of the Goth Pelayo, incorruptible by bribe, indomitable in belief and courage.

A legend tells how a hermit lived in the cave, guarding the image of the Virgin from the Moorish despoilers. Some evil-doer, pursued by Pelayo's vengeance, took refuge in the cave, followed by the king. The hermit, pleading that the fugitive had taken sanctuary beneath the Virgin's protection, asked pardon for him from the Goth, as one day he himself might need that very shelter and defence. Pelayo pardoned the criminal, and the hermit, filled with the spirit, prophesied the victory which should be to the Christians in Covadonga.

It is probable that the refuge was an ancient one, and that such relics and images as were kept here were brought by the fugitives themselves. When Morales came up the valley in 1572 he wrote: 'One of the points which has appeared most noteworthy to me in all this about Covadonga and the district is, that in this place occurred the fury of the war of Augustus Caesar with the Asturians, whom he conquered in the same year in which our Redeemer was born. It thus appears that they sheltered in the natural fastnesses of Covadonga and its surroundings, so one can understand that this place was well known as a sanctuary in the days of Pelayo, since others had taken refuge there before them. There is here in the valley a memorial of the time of Augustus Caesar, in a place called Coras, above which is the church of Santa Eulalia, where old people saw more than twenty stones of Roman tombs which have now been used up in building so that only three remain. Also the Aras Sextianas, which, as all Roman histories say, remain for memorial of that victory in Asturias, are no more than four or five leagues from this valley.'

To the cave in Covadonga, then, fled Pelayo, prince of the

blood royal, with three hundred men. The Arab historian Rasis (translated from the Spanish of Don Carlos Quirós Rodríguez) is definite on the incident which changed the future of Spain. 'In the days of Ambasa-ben-Sohain El Kelbí there rose in the country of Galicia a nefarious barbarian called Pelayo, in whose time the Christians began to gather power enough in Spain (reinforced by the Eastern Christians, the Franks) to seize from the Muslims that which they held in their grasp, since they did not look upon their dominion with favourable eyes. For in Spain the Muslims had subjugated the Christians, expelling them and taking possession of their lands as far as Narbonne in the country of the Franks and conquering even to Pamplona of Galicia. There remained nothing more than a rocky mountain in which there took refuge a king called Pelayo. Here he entered with three hundred men, never ceasing to fight with the Muslims, until his followers died of hunger, leaving no more than thirty men and ten women, whose only food was honey which they gathered in the crevices of the rock, and on this honey they sustained life. Weary of this attitude the Muslims depreciated them, saying "From thirty men what evil can come to us?"'

Anyone brought up on the Old Testament begins to suspect the issue when easy potentates talk in this manner of 'a contemptible remnant' in the mountains. Left in some freedom, then, Pelayo and his thirty men were joined by increasing numbers, until, rumours reaching the ruling Muslims of some stirring of Christians in the Asturian valleys, an army was sent to deal with the matter and put an end to it (A.D. 718). Pelayo was to be seduced, if possible, by promises of good to himself by the time-serving Bishop Oppas, who came with the troops of Mahomet, and, if still unyielding, the affair was to be concluded by battle. The rout of the over-confident Moors makes one of the epics of Spain. That Berber warriors who possessed a mountain country like that of Atlas should be at a loss in the hill passes seems not very credible. But Pelayo and his people were in the heights of their own mountains, and waging warfare after their own tradition. The Moors were broken and fled towards Liébana, when there occurred one of those landslides or earthquakes which visit a mountain country in times of heavy rains and swollen torrents. Many were buried, others swept away by the flooded river, and the kingdom of Asturias was won. The royal house established itself at Gijón. The cave was remembered as a sanctuary, and the wooden chapel seen by Morales was built in front of it by Alfonso I, who founded the monastery in the eighth century, carrying out, as he said, in all this, the express wishes of his predecessor Pelayo.

The earlier chapel, held out from the mouth of the cave on beams of yew above the waterfall, is described by Ambrosio Morales. A print of this chapel, probably from contemporary description, shows a Noah's Ark above a deluge of waters, with stairways of wood as if up to heaven. 'Chapel of the miracle', it seemed to the sagacious old Father that a miracle was continued daily in its suspension above the torrent. The belief urged upon him that it was miraculously preserved by God from decay, being the same chapel as originally built, he dismisses dryly with the comment, 'God no doubt can do even greater things than this, but I saw everywhere evidences of new work and not of the date of that monarch!' (739–757).

Between air and water as it was, it was by fire that the chapel was finally destroyed.

A small wooden chapel now covers the altar of the 'Virgin

of battles' on the floor of the cave, the worshippers having for roof the overhanging rocks.

This chapel, designed as a citadel, with every known Visigothic detail laboriously copied and assimilated from the small knowledge remaining of such churches in the country, has a small interest other than its somewhat perfunctory architecture. When all such details are gathered together, how intensely Oriental is the interior! Does the deduction lead one then to the conclusions of M. Dieulafoy that Persia was the wellspring of the Visigothic fountain? It is interesting to notice by the way.

Hugging the cliff and close beneath the cave the cloister of the monastery founded by Alfonso I was rebuilt in the sixteenth century. On either side of the small mortuary chapel in the cloister are two remarkable Visigothic tombs unexplained by historians. Each sarcophagus lies in the wall, richly carved with flat geometrical patterns—stars, roundels—arrow-head ornament—diapers—on the lid and the front. An arch bearing a sculptured border of stars covers the recess, which has the wall beneath it decorated with flat panels of geometric carving. Beneath one of the tombs are three brackets with grotesque animal heads, possibly lions, more Romanesque than Visigothic—and in this tomb the symmetry of the geometric ornament is broken by two panels, one bearing the figure of a man on horseback, the other the 'Cross of Victory'. This cross, seen in the Cámara Santa at Oviedo, was carried or raised by Pelayo at the battle of Covadonga and later decorated with jewels by Alfonso I. The valleys of Covadonga are now the national park of Spain, the clear airs and cascading green of its woods making it a happy place of pilgrimage. The new church, built at great cost, on an abrupt peak thrust sheer into the valley, like a votive church held high on a mighty hand, is finely enough designed for its situation. The material is good (though its furniture is deplorably commonplace) and if the work has a perfunctoriness which gives a chill, the mountain weather may be trusted to acclimatize it to something more venerable. From the valley it leads the eye satisfactorily to the heights of this 'cradle' full of fierce bright sun and high austere rocks, in which the valour of a race was cherished and its faith fulfilled.

Chapter Twenty-six

THE LIÉBANA

THE LIÉBANA

Above the forests of Monte Viorna which dominate the valleys of the Liébana a gigantic cross on the summit guides the traveller in the mountains to the monastery of Santo Toribio, built far beneath it in a fold of the precipice to guard the relic of the 'True Cross' brought by Santo Toribio from Jerusalem in the year 783, the seventy-second year of the Moorish occupation. Under the mighty hills the tiny belfry which sends its summons from a small eminence into two valleys at one time looks like a stag scenting the morning for danger. To-day, at the sound, the peasants from distant valleys are climbing the hill road on their ponies and donkeys to venerate the 'True Cross' as they have done for six hundred years. Closing the valley at the other end is the great bulk of the Peña Sagra, the first summit to lose the light of the evening, but the first to receive the sunrise in the morning. On its slopes stands the chapel of 'Our Lady of the Light'. Another day there will be the same long file of asses and ponies and people to the little sanctuary. For the mountain people are tenacious of their sanctities. Above la Liébana stand the Picos de Europa, sanctuary, shield, and nucleus of the Christian recovery in Spain. The breastplate of Spain, sharp with defences as the targe of ancient Scotland—against which every invader broke his strength, this indomitable range yet rises to no great height. Some 9000 feet merely, the Picos thrust their sun-gashed crags into the morning with such superb and gleaming armoury of war (dropping veil after veil in the heat), with such unlikeness in their savage sterility to the cultivation and soft vineyards of the valleys, that, like the Coolins of Skye, they impress by their very dissimilarity to the country above which they have always lifted their stony invincible shield, guarding in spirit and seclusion whatever unconquerable element still remained in a dauntless and waiting people. Far below the naked peaks, forests cling like shadows to the high slopes—woods of holly-trees are there, beneath which the deer, taking shelter in winter, are easily snared by the hunters. Bears and wolves and wild boars and the lynx live up there with the eagles and the storms which are now the chief enemies of the vineyards of Liébana. 'The Liébanese smile more than they laugh, but it may be a smile lasts longer', writes a lover of La Montaña. But from the attentive and watchful attitudes of danger, the valleys now have rest. Only here and there the hidden position of a monastery crouching beneath a precipice in a profound valley, the presence of a fortified house, the still earlier and ruder keep of a dismantled castle, give a grave architectural reminder of a stirring and warlike history. The little town of Potes (reached by a State road begun by Ferdinand VI and Barbara of Braganza to open a way for the flour of Castile to the sea-coast, which has served to carry the wood for the arsenals of Spain from the forests of Liébana) lies beneath the Picos de Europa—bearing in its architecture the history and developments of many a mountain town, a road which enters seclusions between mountain walls more like cañons than a pass.

Twice a week it suffers a major and minor commotion. On Monday the rocky steep streets clatter with the picking of the feet of mules and asses; and the slow bell of the draught oxen drawing wicker chariots shaped like that of an ancient Pompeian and jolting on two solid wooden wheels tolls its heavy passage. On this day of the market the population of the valleys for miles comes into the town for its week's provisions, making evident the importance and number of shops in this small central town of Liébana.

On market day, too, when everybody comes with horse and ass, the shabby and closed ground stories of so many mountain houses are explained. For now these stand open and their use as stables for mules and ponies and the talkative donkeys is apparent. Only on the first floor does the living-place begin for the family, and the shabbiness of the streets of many small towns of the mountains is to be explained by the fact that room has to be found for the saddle-beasts so indispensable on the hill journeys. Passed the folk and their beasts from the town, and the smell of ordure lifted from the streets, Potes becomes a quiet town with a history. The history of mountain architecture, whose development one can trace in a town so important as Potes, has been very carefully and efficiently written by Señor Don Elías Ortiz de la Torre, and it is in some sense the history of most mountain peoples. There was the early rough life of the clan gathered round the feudal lord in his castle (hard and savage as that of Highland Scotland), in the days of war and persecution both refuge and citadel. As more and more of the Christian remnant were driven to the mountains they, living ever on the alert, built their houses closed and often fortified. The persecution, too, explains the number of monasteries and churches in places difficult of access, since a whole remnant had to be gathered and hidden. The absence of the patio, which was Moorish, and the presence of the tower and the *solana* are accounted for. Then came the easier days of the Reconquest when, with the discovery of artillery, the tower became obsolete as defence and was used to give importance to a lordly house—its battlements gradually softening in outline to pierced or pointed balustrades. Plateresque varied taste. With the Renaissance came Herrera, the greatest and latest important influence on the seignorial house, himself of the Montaña. Baroque passed by, and now there is the modern rediscovery of the regional house of the mountains and the modern dispute between the convenient and the picturesque.

Spaciousness, strength, and a kind of self-containedness inherited from dangerous and remote times characterize the mountain houses. In old houses the actual windows are little more than peep-holes giving an air of secrecy to a high stone façade. The *solana* is very large and is a delightful feature of the North, being in effect a wide upper room with the front wall left out and in its place a carved wooden balcony, often highly ornamental—a dry, sunny, spacious place in the upper part of the house. Or there is the balcony proper under enormous eaves projecting far enough to give complete shelter to the entire width, the eaves themselves often forming 'dove-cotes' for pigeons. The inn 'El Comercio' at Potes is a fine type of such a house—with the houses immediately round it.

It is September and the vintage is beginning in the valleys —everywhere the fruits, so abundant and good, are being gathered, and the almond and walnut and chestnut-trees beaten for their nuts. The men are cutting the branches of the poplars for winter fodder, and there remain only tender green fronds swaying on the tall stems. There is no lack of company in the fields. Wine-casks are being washed and rolled into the streets to dry. The autumn crocus is covering the stubble places with the lavender of sunset peaks. 'Quita-meriendas', the country people call these flowers, that is, 'leave your daytime snacks'. There is always time to eat after dark and the daylight gets shorter after the blossoming of the crocus. In the evening we climb the road to the monastery of Santo Toribio, once of such grandeur and importance—and now, its living-places abandoned to charcoal-burners and shepherds, the guardian of its relic and church a young priest little more than a boy. All the pyrotechnics of all the sunsets of eighteenth-century guide-books went with us on our road under the Picos. Superlatives ebbed from our speech, and silence was the best tribute to the amazing panorama. The monastery itself, hidden until one is close upon it, had passed through many changes even before Morales chron-icled its treasures and its library. If it were founded by the Santo Toribio of the fifth century it must be the earliest in Spain. If by the later Bishop of Palencia of that name it is still a very venerable foundation. But of the early Roman-esque buildings there is chiefly dilapidation. Hens roost and pigs grub in the old monastery kitchens, and the big gate-way is filled with sacks of charcoal to keep out the wind. The present church of transition Gothic has the seventeenth-

House of the Marquis, Santillana del Mar

The River and Cathedral, Pamplona

century chapel which holds the reliquary of the 'Lignum Crucis' as a transept. This, pleasantly Baroque, is kept in good repair and visited every Friday for the veneration of the Cross by peasants from the whole district. Two magnificent pieces of Córdoba leather hang as altar-frontals in the main church (one having suffered from the thieving pen-knife of a visitor), but this is all that remains apparent of ancient honour and prestige. The distressing scrub which grows upon the felling of great trees covers the mountainsides, but the private purchase of forest is, I hear, in the valley, being discouraged by the State. If a town needs a fountain or a public benefaction, so many trees are marked and felled—but under restriction, and the replanting is now, I think, being done. So that the depletion of the forests which Ford bewailed has the attention of the Spaniard. 'Whoever loves Liébana must make himself the apostle of the tree!' Coming down from the platform of the belfry in the solemn and tragic evening light we met the priest, a pleasant and kindly boy with his hat on the back of his head, striding up the road to his lonely post on the hill.

'Had we seen the relic? Ah no!' He slapped his cassock. 'He had the keys in his pocket!'

On the slopes a shepherd boy was scrambling after his sheep, singing as though all Spain was his own. Now and then the shepherd's voice joined with him and the tinkling of the sheep-bells ran like a brook on the hill. The *grillos* trilled till the mountain rang, so tiny a creature waking miniature echoes! The Picos rose higher as the sun set, formidable, majestic. Tragic and mournful the light drifted away, and the Picos became shadows, awful, but far off. 'Now the Picos are so clear one could find an English dictionary upon them' is an observation that will make a Spaniard laugh in Potes.

For there lies a curiosity in the shop of Señor Bustamante, the watchmaker, which is English as his clock. Looking up at the peaks scarred with myriad crevices one knows how even a man might be lost and not found. But up there at some time went an Englishman who dropped a dictionary the size of a postage stamp—Bryce's English Dictionary, printed by Robert MacLehose of Glasgow and dedicated to 'Mrs Kendal who has the largest collection of miniature books in existence'—and this, the smallest of printed works, was picked up in the Picos de Europa by the indefatigable climber and citizen of Potes.

A song, always the same melody, now fills the valleys every evening. From one side of the hill or another, women descend, their baskets on their heads, singing as they return from work in the now empty vineyards. They sing the harvest song of the vintage, heard only once a year.

SANTA MARÍA DE LEBEÑA

Where corn is carried high on the mountains and forests crowd to the utmost vertical crags; among the chestnut-trees, in a profound valley with the river Deva rushing like wind in the poplars, where white mountain walls hold up a blue heaven as a canopy above a secret and sacred mystery, the little Mozárabe church of Santa María de Lebeña stands, one of the most beautiful monuments of Christian Spain. A yew and an olive grow on either side; the pueblo of Lebeña— '200 souls' says the priest—straggles above; the mountains give back, not ominous in their strength, but white, and as it were, revealing a little place containing wonders.

The learned and scholarly work of Professor Gómez Moreno on the Mozárabe churches of Spain gives all the architect and student can know of modern research, but for general readers the Mozárabe churches (few in number and many of the few having suffered transformation) were those built by the Mozárabe population—that is, the Christian population living under Moorish dominion. Caught, as it were, and surrounded by the Moorish net, where this subject population were allowed to build places for their worship, they carried on the tradition familiar to them as Christian, from material left in the country by the Visigoths, but, from their enclosed position and the prevalence within it of Moorish builders and architects, gradually assimilated ideas of decoration and ornament and solutions of construction from the dominant Moorish class. From the South came the Berber invasion, cutting short further Christian development, and later from the North came the powerful influences from France and the Romanesque style of building which was to fix on the Christian provinces of Spain a style in which she expressed her own temper happily and with dignity.

Of these early Mozárabe churches Santa María de Lebeña is one of the earliest and most complete. At first sight, from the bridle-path under the walnut-trees, the tower and the portico give one the impression of a Florentine church in an Apennine valley. But near at hand the high roof of the Asturian tradition (the portico being a seventeenth-century addition and the tower designedly new and apart that there may be no confusion in later years for the architectural student) and the bands of flat ornament familiar in these early churches, the richly carved brackets of stone which support the wide eaves (brackets worked like the ironing-boards of the early Norwegian peasantry), prepare one for the extraordinary interior beauty of this mountain survival. From outside the building is like a collection of small high apartments each with a separate roof and each rising higher towards the middle, the whole like a pyramid with wide steps.

Inside one wonders how such a massive and grand effect could have been built into so tiny a space. The central roof is very high, as in all these churches, over a basilica, and the fourfold columns, from each of which a heavy Visigothic horseshoe arch (this traditional arch of the Visigothic period of building is other than that of the Moorish architects and often gives date and origin to these Spanish churches) springs in different directions, are unusually strong and simple. That is all, and yet the effect is of a great and noble church. One can only admire the wonderful sense of proportion and loftiness of architectural ambition in these early Spanish builders. Señor Lampérez sees Santa María de Lebeña as nearer to the Asturian churches than the Mozárabe, and the fourfold columns on their square bases as showing Romanesque forms before true Romanesque was fully awake.

The story of the building of the church in the valley is told in the history of the districts of Liébana by a writer in *La Voz de Liébana*. The authority of the mountain province being in the hands of a certain nephew of Ordoño I called Alfonso, this prince resolved to take the body of Santo Toribio from the monastery which bears his name and build a small shrine for it in his own principality. But when the soldiers began to dig, both the evil prince and the innocent soldiers were struck with blindness, which blindness continued until the custody of the Saint was confirmed to the monks and great benefices pertaining to the prince were also handed to them, together with the church of Santa María de Lebeña, now an offering of expiation on behalf of the repentant Alfonso.

Simple people accommodate themselves very happily on old battle-grounds while quarrels shrivel in archives. What remains to the sight now in the valley surrounded by white crags and mountain walls is a little parish church of unusual design and another national monument for Spain.

'*Plan, columns, system of equilibrium, arches, capitals, all is ours* [i.e. *Spanish*] *and all tends towards a complete architectural style—a style already in process of unfolding itself to more splendid things. There is nothing in Western Europe which could possibly have served as a model*' (LAMPÉREZ).

Chapter Twenty-seven

SAN VICENTE DE LA BARQUERA

When Charles V sailed into the harbour of San Vicente de la Barquera to take formal possession of the country of Spain, historic incident was supplied with a fair background. Even a world-emperor must have been pleased with the beauty of the land which was to be his. How often, sailing past the coast of Spain, one has guessed at the possibilities of the alluring and secret sands shining from the land far out to sea. And now one knows. A tiny place, this ancient *villa* of Cantabria, which was once important enough to receive an emperor coming for a crown, its history silted up as is the bar of its once humming port. The entrance from the open sea is so narrow that the importance of its shelter might easily have been missed by an enemy. Two imposing bridges carry a fine road in and out of the town, skirting the outer harbour. Behind them, within the indented tidal creeks which were the shipbuilding yards of the time of the Admiral

Bonifaz who broke the bridge of the Moorish boats at Seville in the days of Ferdinand I, are sluggish waters detained within dykes—the remains of five harbours of San Vicente, their entrances secret and obscure, known only to those who had business there—a Scapa Flow of Spain. For only in these northern parts could the preparations of the Spaniard be free from the observation of the Moor. The importance of the north for the freedom of the south was a point missed by the prosperous invader. Standing about the bay are the mountains which held the 'remnant which should return', gathering strength in their secure and lofty hiding-places to thrust and to push and to possess finally the country of their patrimony. In the early September morning the Picos de Europa shine in the height of heaven, visionary as mountains of the future, displayed by some revealing angel to the first Adam of the garden. Across the long bridge of twenty-eight arches every traveller has the importance of an incident. The small stone house, lit on one side, with its solitary tree at the entrance of the bridge, has the seriousness and interest of a human dwelling on a lonely highland shore.

'If this were in America or Cuba it would be a great harbour', said the dueño of the Fishermen's Guild. 'But here there is no one to do it.' Coming from Bilbao one is not sorry there is no one to do it, for minerals taken out of the earth take a sad revenge upon its surface. And if 'recent history has a bitter taste like unripe fruit', history that is so safely over that the stark wall of a castle, one seignorial house, a noble church built for a larger and more populous *villa* than the present, are all that climb the hammer-headed hill above the five harbours where Charles V, being made free of Spain, saw the hidalgos fight the first bull-fight as gentlemen did in those days—proving their mettle before their sovereign—shows rather like a picture-book in this landscape of old Cantabria. Merchants lived here once and shipbuilders, and the town had a Jews' Quarter. Here lived the family of the Archbishop of Seville in Isabella's day— the Inquisitor Corro, who came back to San Vicente to die. His tomb, made in Genoa, is the chief treasure of a noble church with Romanesque doors. It lies in the chapel of his ancestors, next to that of his father and mother, and shows the figure of a man reclining, his head raised and supported on his hand, in the act of reading. The face of beauty and birth has the calm of a man who saw a straight path before him—no conflict, almost no thought. Beside him lie the father and mother from whom he inherited his beauty. There, in this place of fishermen, the still standing façade of the house of this family with its coat of arms is one of two illuminated letters of the tattered archive of San Vicente.

But it was the merchant and builder who made the prosperity of the first of the four *villas* of the Sea of Cantabria. The imposing castle dominating the harbour was more used for merchant purposes and for custom dues than for defence, says the historian. On three sides of the plaza, round its plantation of bleached acacia-trees, there is a wide street beneath a dark arcade—shelter both from sun and wind. The old houses are packed right together, going back to a great depth. One begins to see how the town might have been humming and thriving in the Middle Ages. Then came two great fires—plague—wars—the loss of commerce—the silting-up of the harbours, and history lay on its side and went to sleep. Past history makes a fine flourish, but there is something more gracious in recording the present. Passing down the street we were invited (with the simplicity one finds so often in small Spanish towns) to visit the *Círculo*.

Here it is the Guild of Fishermen. In a long dim room leading from the street to the double arcade on the harbour front
is the 'House of the Fishermen'. Tables for coffee and
dominoes, a small platform for lectures, and a library!—a
small square room partitioned off the corner farthest away
from talk. The books are gifts, histories of navigation—bio-
logical works, the *Scientific American*. At the table some boys
were studying hard. The Guardia Civil was reading too.
'You will see', he said, 'that most of the books are of technical
interest to sailors and men interested in ships.'

But when the blue summer tide brings the fishing boats
over the bar, intelligence is awake (or is it a beautiful landscape in a beautiful autumn?) of a sudden moment before
sundown, on an evening when the reflections in soundless
water seem as substantial as the castle fading in the vaporous
sunlight of heat. The 'summits of Europe' appear mighty
and silent as a reminder in the heights, the tide climbs over
the sand-locked bar with effort and complaint, and San
Vicente has the appearance of some old coloured picture—
the entrance to something magical and secret, its two bridges
carrying the world past it on either side—its history like the
obliterated fresco on a village church wall, of which one
deciphers now only the foot and hand of a warrior, the
mantle of a rider flying in the wind. The wanness of mountain twilight falls on the secret harbours of San Vicente. The
bell sounds for the Rosary. A wail goes over the fields—
'Mar-í-a! Mar-í-a!' for somebody's María always gets lost
at this time of evening in Spain. On the harbour wall the
light streams out from under the arcade of the 'Fishermen's
House'. On the bar one hears the beating of Atlantic tides.

Chapter Twenty-eight

THE ASTURIAN COAST

CUDILLERO

If Santillana, from which the sea is three miles distant, has become a 'sleeping town' of Spain, Cudillero, on the sea, is as animated and awake as a net full of fish just drawn to shore. Whoever thought of hanging houses on the face of a cliff and propping them underneath with pillars and stairs, and filling the sides of a chasm with a town so that it barely holds on by its eyebrows above the crack of tide which is its harbour, had no thought of the picturesque in making, but how it has been achieved! Coloured and comical as Naples, but with a more immediate intimacy with the sea than any great seaport can command, it buzzes in the crack of cliff letting out to the sea, like a sandpit full of martins. The narrowness of its vertical cliff walls must make life there rather like life in a series of city flats. Do fishermen's wives do more washing than other people? For from every window and balcony of Cudillero coloured garments were flapping like banners to welcome the home-coming boats. The curious long boats of the Biscay fishermen were making port as we went down, drawing up along a slant from the harbour like 'Buckler's Hard'. Girls with small barrels of fish on their heads were climbing upwards like processions of slaves bearing gifts to potentates. Under the cliff which catches the sun, the drying-poles, thick and high as forest trees, make an avenue along the sea-wall. The nets, heavier than the herring-nets of the west of Scotland, have a closer mesh. The boats are long like the northern boats of Scandinavia. Files of fishermen walk with a passing subtlety of colour along the pale jetty, dragging in each hand the great silver and black *bonitos* (tunnies) of the catch. Behind them, on the shoulders of four boys, the heavy brown nets are carried like tribute. Who would believe that the solemn whirlpool of mountains which brings the State road through the pass to Pravia had such a fluttering ejaculation at its exit!

It must be a difficult harbour to make, one imagines, when the fog lies thick on the Biscay coast. For the life of the Biscay fisherman is not like that of the Mediterranean sailor —'deep water, no fog'—but more like that of the fishers of our own fog-haunted coast. It is pleasant to know that the needs of the fisherman have been sympathetically observed by the higher ranks at sea, and that hostels for the men are being placed, as money and help are forthcoming, along the shores of that difficult northern coast. These houses are proving to be the very refuge and comfort which was the earnest intention of that good admiral their founder.

Chapter Twenty-nine

SANTILLANA DEL MAR
AND ALTAMIRA

SANTILLANA DEL MAR

In Spain I have many admirations but three tendernesses:
one for the primitive churches of the Asturias, a second
for the Plateresque cloister, and a third for the Renaissance
palaces; and to find within the folded antiquity of a green
Downland near the sea, with the sweetness of atmosphere
which that great laver insists upon in its neighbourhood, a
red-roofed town of the palaces of my heart, is to find as rare
a thing as Wisby in Gothland.

To come through the early August morning, its pale sky
empty and ready for heat, but holding in the dawn a core
of coolness precious as a frosty dew, and to enter this ancient

capital of the Asturias, this *pueblo dormido* of modern Spain, this town of honey-coloured palaces closed in by green hills, whose first feudal lord was a classic poet and courtier, is like opening the faded velvet covers of an old vellum chronicle. Not the history, but the quality of an epoch, lingers in a gesture, airs for musicians, quarrels, jests, contests of poets, which stir now no regret, nor wish to see them start to life about one. 'They are all grass on the threshing-floor', sighs Don Jorge Manrique. 'The tourneys and joustings, the banners and trappings and gilding. Where are the deeds of King John and the Knights of Aragón? Phantoms which faded and passed.' But he was near enough to remember and regret. The English habit of absorbing history within the usefulness of daily life has left few of these sleeping towns within her counties. Winchelsea, perhaps, and it may be Rye, are like shells in which the rumour of distant tides now murmurs.

As so often happens in Spain, one never expects to find anything so rare, so unassertive, as this ancient town of Santillana. Summer jasmine, the scent of ripe maize fields, and the leisure of the country penetrate and fill its streets, two long streets leading to the Romanesque collegiate church of a twelfth-century monastic settlement. Sometimes, as at Betanzos, one finds a town whose situation one knows at once must be very ancient. Just within that confluence of hills, just on that eminence beside a river, would be the place of encampment for an army of occupation. But though quarrels were once tossed like gloves through the streets of Santillana, the gentle slope of its hills, the wide valleys inviting cultivation, show the older and more pacific intentions of the churchmen round whose powerful establishment the township gradually gathered.

In England the suggestion of a mellow and gracious domestic exterior stirs the memories of Virginia creeper on old red-brick houses in country cathedral towns. But in Spain it is the gracious turn which the Renaissance took when it left its preoccupation with ecclesiastical architecture, and drew within its atmosphere the daily life of the high-bred Spaniard, which warms the eye like sunlight. The glowing and tender quality of old sandstone, honey-coloured and fine in surface, the cornices so deep that the shadows hang like mats on the sun-tinctured walls, the spaciousness and shade in the courtyards, the discretion and richness of the decorated façade, lie in the enchantment of antiquity as in a sunny sleep. Here, as in Oviedo, one recognizes the beautiful substance which stone itself can be, and there is always something in the Spanish liking for massiveness of structure which takes away from the facile picturesque. The simplicity of the Colegiata at the town's end stands up well to the simple shape and lighting of the hills with a dignity which even the romanticism of its deep colour does not make trivial. Sometimes the façade of a whole palace depends for its enrichment upon the use of the escudo, whose value as an ornament is thus increased by the solitariness of its position. Ornament used sparingly as to its distribution, but with magnificence where it is applied upon the face of a palace of massive proportion and simplicity of building, gives the impression of a mental outlook which is stately rather than easy. A little unmanageable, perhaps, the Renaissance found the Spaniard, having obviously ideas of his own. From house to house antiquity leads backwards, but the eyeless Gothic façade of the 'house of Gil Blas' is the oldest, the shadow of its tower seeming as substantial as its building, the tower too grey and old for the sunshine to make any pretence of gilding it, and where even the weeds clinging to its edges have the colour of immortelles. Almost in the manner of a fort it dominates the road to the Colegiata, whose stately group, a little aloof, more venerable than the palaces by which it was dispossessed, has an air of belonging to the valley which the palaces have never acquired. The unusually spacious cloister has an air of desertion which only a collegiate church seems to know. No disused monastery ever gathers quite so forsaken an atmosphere. From centuries of the friction of churchmen, the intrigues of nobles, the preposterous splendours and quarrels of an epoch, there remains a village church and a classic poet for Spain.

Something like Orcagna's fresco, 'The Song of Life'; like the ladies in the gardens of a French book of hours, formal, arranged, high bred, and delicate, are the poems of the Marqués of Santillana,[1] first feudal lord of this first Asturian capital, who introduced the sonnet into Spanish letters and who sounded the few and ringing notes of the troubadour with a very engaging freshness.

The acrimonies and angers in which he shared no longer disturb. But the *serranillas*, gallantries without tears, delicate

---

[1] Marqués de Santillana. Iñigo Lopez de Mendoza (1398–1458), created Marqués de Santillana, 1445, after the battle of Olmedo. He was a poet and patron of letters and introduced the sonnet form into Spanish verse. A free translation of the Spanish verse quoted (which is from a much longer poem) is as follows:

> 'With masterly music,
> He sang this song,
> Which caused my heart
> To lose all its fears:
> "Fittingly should I extol Love,
> Since everywhere
> It has turned my heaviness
> Into gaiety."'

encounters in the country, the figures of ladies and courtiers stepping to gay music, as formal as a minuet and as serious (if the troubadour laughs he is lost), delight the sensitive ear with their burden.

> Por música e maestría
> Cantava esta cançión,
> Que fizo a mi coraçón
> Perder el pavor que avía:
> Bien devo loar amor
> Pues todavía
> Quiso tornar mi tristor
> En alegría.

Into the little town something still older than clerics or soldiers has crept back and taken possession. The farms of the valleys have their centre in Santillana. The chief sounds in the streets are those of the farmyard. Cows and asses and mules live in the lower story of the palaces in the patriarchal way—part of the family. Passing when the doors are open one sees stables as vast and cool and dark as caverns with the motionless silhouettes of oxen and mules in the dusky interior. Morning and evening the street is full of the soft tramp of cows coming for water. There is the splash of a pail; the call to driven animals; the clatter of a mule; the quick step of a donkey carrying fodder or Indian corn. The voices which linger are those of women about the fountain. The voices which pass out beyond into the fields are those of men. 'Aquí, Señora, no hay nada más que antigüedad', said a woman as I passed. 'Only those who are interested in antiquity come to Santillana.'

'ART IS LONG'

I do not remember that any artist has ever written upon the painted cave of Altamira in Old Castile. The savant has had it in his care now for some years, and by minute and meticulous methods of observation and analysis has arrived at most interesting conclusions and comparisons; but not from the standpoint of the painter or the artist's special approach to *his* objective.

It is quite probable that the primitive man of 25,000 years ago thought in just such a way, and required the pictures for precisely such urgencies as are attributed to him by the learned. But the actual man who *devised the method of doing it* (for whatever purpose such pictorial presentations were needed) is also of the greatest significance. What alone survives from all the activities of this prehistoric race is their art, and the method of arriving at pictures which the primitive artist used is of a very lively interest. For *his* mind, it is evident, on examination of the paintings, explored along the ways which the same sort of mind to-day only widens and deepens and makes credible, and what is absorbing now to the artist who follows is not his divergence but the similarity of his approach to his problem. Art, it seems, never changes its intention, any more than life does; and these paintings of Altamira, virtually from another planet (for after the passage of 25,000 years it must certainly be another planet now revolving), must have been accomplished, as the methods of working show, by just the same processes of thought and deduction as similar works to-day.

One thing is disclosed as one examines the 'Sistine Chapel of primitive man', and that is the sum of the knowledge visible, both in primitive chemistry (or whatever stood for such) and in actual art experience. The men who painted the cave of Altamira were certainly not beginners in art. They were the Michael Angelos and Raphaels of their day, having reached probably all the art-knowledge possible to their degree of civilization, being in possession of all the technical means open to them for the expression of such knowledge.

Sometimes the paintings of children form a convenient parallel for comparison with the art of primitive peoples. There is the child's ability to catch and reproduce a gesture (if it has not been taught how to do it). There is the sum of a child's observation; the sort of thing it notices; the way in which it will attempt an impossibility and by reason of its desire to do it arrive at an astonishing result. But except for the common artist-ability to preserve the child's faculty of naïve observation into maturity (the combination of *naïveté* and experience being the two impulses of art achievement), I do not believe these artists of primitive man to have been in this sense children. The child-quality is present in the Altamira paintings, but more settled and important is the mature and consistent knowledge displayed.

This oblong chamber between two shelves of rock deep in the heart of the hill was an apartment dedicated ultimately to some use dissociated from domestic life, and the highest available skill was brought to its ornamentation. The pigments are, of course, earth pigments, and limited in range to such colours as exist in pure earth—sanguine, black (probably from soot), and orange. They were mixed and made to adhere by means of animal fat. For 25,000 years or more water has percolated through the rock from the fields outside, and yet the colours remain. Tiny pieces of coloured substance are found from time to time, the primitive artist's palette. Hollow bones from which the marrow was extracted and, having been mixed with colour, returned to its original receptacle, and formed thus a tube of moist colour, and mortars for pounding and mixing colours, have been discovered, and it is probable that the tufted tails of animals suggested a pliable means of applying colour by brushes, the use of which was certainly known to the artist of Altamira.

There was intentional and careful preparation of the upper ledge or ceiling of the cave for the pictures to be painted. Incomplete paintings show the smoothing and scraping preparation and the scratching with flints for the outline and detail. But it is the manner of the very free and accomplished brushwork and the skilful use and knowledge of the use of curves in the drawing which show our advanced artist at work, and which disclose that the cave painter was at the summit of the available art-information of his age.

When the ambassadors of Montezuma met Cortés with presents, the Spanish soldiers pointed out to the Conquistador the presence of certain men among the Aztecs who were making rapid drawings of the Spaniards, their horses, their arms, their demeanour, as the quickest way to convey to Montezuma the quality of the invaders. And one savant suggested that the paintings of Altamira 'anticipated instantaneous photography', the picture of a horse galloping, not with legs outstretched, but with legs gathered up under him, recalling modern effects with the kinema.

But the mental processes of the artists were precisely the reverse. It was not, as in the case of Montezuma's Aztecs, to *write* in pictures and convey information that the artist of Altamira pounded his colours. The pictures of Altamira were to express some primitive imagination, and were to remain static, and they do in fact convey something of the mental process by which the civilized Chinese arrived at their highly conventionalized art. The freedom of the curves, the rhythm of one attitude, one gesture conveyed without interruption, make clear that the drawing was memory-drawing as in the case of the Chinese. The line is not disturbed by the necessity of raising the eyes to the object to be portrayed. One gesture has been closely observed and set down from memory, disturbing details having no place because unremembered, the whole simplified and rhythmical because the object is not present to the sight. In the very careful reconstructions of the paintings done by the Abbé Breuil there is one peculiarity which he has not been able to convey (though he adds careful diagrammatic statements of the fact), and that is the unevenness of the surface of the rock upon which the animals are painted. The paintings even contain a groping after sculpture. The excrescences and inequalities of the rock ceiling have been constantly used to form the hunched flank of a recumbent bison, the bending neck of a cow, the turned head of a deer. Manes of hair are scratched deeply in the rock by flints first, and the colour last applied to the pictured imagination. For whatever purpose this interior chamber was used, whether for banquet, religious rite, or entombment, it discovers an extraordinary degree of skill and artistic invention; and what a light deposit of earth and stones has hidden it from knowledge for 25,000 years! An inquisitive little dog groping for rabbits makes it known, and a little girl looking for nothing in particular, and therefore at liberty to use her eyes, joyfully shouts her discovery of *toros* (bulls) on the painted ceiling. A romantic discovery, truly, under these hills of Castile, with the suave green covering and gentle folding of the South Downs, with their hay-scented breeze and soft sea mist, at the end of a safe and ancient valley rustling with maize harvest, this painted chamber in the security of the hill. For whatever purpose it was once used it remains now the memorial chamber of a race of men whose only permanence was their art.

Chapter Thirty

DURANGO AND BILBAO

DURANGO

In a landscape much like any other mountain country are set those large farms with immense roofs, those vast church porticos, and those strange rude carvings of Vizcaya. One has no need to go farther than Durango to find all three in one small and cheerful town among maize fields, with green hills swept by sweet summer rains and a river running clear and rapid from the highlands.

The Portico of Durango is built on to the side of the church of Santa María and for a long time one gets no farther into the town for wondering at the gigantic scale of these church porticoes, which, attached to the church, yet belong to the township and serve as market-places—massive and lofty as the granaries of ancient monasteries, conveying something of the exaggeration of size by which early artists

[226]

of travel brought home their impressions of magnitude. The Portico of Santiago in Bilbao is of the same architectural construction, vaulted like the church, itself of lofty proportion and grand scale. That of Durango, roomy like the market-halls of Flanders or France, has yet a solidity and space purely Spanish. The noble timbers of the roof are like a sustaining forest. The people exchanging the news of the town beneath them are suddenly dwarfed. Like the Hanseatic squares and houses of the north, the portico looks so much too large and impressive for any business that has to be transacted there. Two posts carved like pagodas stand at each entrance for slinging the bridles of mules over. A long stone bench runs round the wall—all so near the ground, beneath that grandiose and powerful conception of a roof.

In the street one finds the Cruz Triaga. This is really the statement of an extraordinary fact, for while the cross is of so singular a character that were a Maya Indian to be converted to Christianity he would find himself completely and happily at home with the form in which his new faith had expressed itself, for a traveller to find this strange carving under the trees of the causeway, like a fountain or a signal-post, is one of the most curious sensations. The Cruz Triaga is a cross of the twelfth century, the four sides of the cross proper carved with the scenes and symbols and persons of the Crucifixion, while round the shaft curls the dragon whose head is lost beneath the persons of the drama on the beam. Beneath a kind of pent-house roof above the Crucified, sun, moon, and angels crowd, giving the air of a totem-pole to this rude, almost savage piece of sculpture.

Through the pretty town with green plazas and resting-places, one comes to the oldest church in Vizcaya, San Pedro de Tavira, on the edge of September maize fields, very lofty, of transition Gothic, with one notable and delightful feature, an elaborately carved gallery-front of grey wood evidently done by some experienced carver. Here too one sees the vast roof of a Vizcayan establishment—as if one great span was made to cover a farmstead. Indeed, from a distance San Pedro looks like a big farm among its maize fields. Here the portico, across whose wide dim space one looks as if from the end of a big English barn, is between the double church on the one side and the inhabited house on the other. The lengthwise, twofold slope covers both church and farm. Square and solid and roomy, the outside wall of the church has a long outer cloister with a sloping roof supported by wooden posts. Some small Romanesque windows remain on this wall, and round the interior walls are a number of charming Romanesque figures set on brackets.

In a village not far from Durango is an assembly of ancient tombstones bearing a singular resemblance to the hog-backed tombs of Govan churchyard near Glasgow.

Chapter Thirty-one

GREEN NAVARRE

It is from the autumn slopes of the Pyrenees, rippling with green, their forests of chestnut-trees and birches, their valleys jewelled with apple orchards, their rains lacing the air with silver and darkening the rivers, that one enters most fitly into green Navarre, once united to England and bearing always some spirit of northern independence in its traditions and story.

These little kingdoms swell with history and heroes. 'To defend these, loving them more than life itself', is a great starting-point for doughty deeds. 'That the kings swear to observe the charter—taking nothing from it—bettering it but making nothing worse and if in any way altering or departing from the law, that act to be null and void', is a peremptory parliamentary gesture to encroaching monarchs. Pamplona itself indeed, with the mass of its fortifications, seems to be guardian for a nation rather than a town. The labyrinth of defences and complicated entrance through a gate with drawbridge and rusty machinery to the south of the town must remain much as Ford saw it a hundred years ago, for when military defences are outmoded what is to be done with them?

One recovers the days of the Crimea among the overgrown ramparts—gun emplacements with rings and pins (still bright) to hold the recoil of the cannon—the elegant tourelles, at the corners of the lower bastions, giving the appearance of the abandoned pleasure gardens of an old French château ruined by war.

Yet there is no monument to warriors in Pamplona. The imaginative side of patriotism is commemorated but not its hammer and machinery. A good modern sculpture of St. Francis, 'peacemaker', who, wandering with two friars to found his Order in Navarre, brought concord into a city divided against itself; a column with the confession of faith in Basque independence. Sarasate and some grey old sovereigns of Navarre, in these, and in the museum arranged with such care in the old Gothic house of the Counts of Navarre, patriotism is as pacific as history that is past and written.

Many cities of Spain show a notable silhouette. In fact, this sky-writing of towers and convents comes at last to be expected by the traveller. But few are so supported by their circumstance as this capital of Navarre. From the sharp angle-bend of the road to Sangüesa the independence of a kingdom builds an imposing architecture against the hills, not without delicate ornament upon its front. Below the glacis poplars crowd like armies, to shelter the river of the strath; the wide valley full of corn fields curves under the hills round the base of the fortifications, and Pamplona stands firm against the

Pyrenees, looking out to France. The ramparts support the mass of the cathedral buildings with impressiveness and force, the two towers take their place with dignity, the delicate loggia and slender height of the chapter-house upon the wall vary the cliff-like descent, the star-pointed bastions below plant a solid base upon the valley, and, like the Grampians across the Carse of Forth from Stirling Castle, the Pyrenees offer their imposing line, hiding whatever may come.

Alert, merry, and clean, the population take a northern pride in their town. One stays to reflect how large a space may be given to the planting of trees for shady gardens in a modern Spanish town, and how the houses are so high that they can spare the lowest floor for the stabling of animals. Old seignorial houses, of the solid northern style with deep eaves and curved balconies, within whose front doors one sees the cobbled entrance which accommodates saddle-horses and mules beneath the grand staircase leading above, are a little obscured in the streets by the height of the ordinary houses and by the habit of painting the whole façade a solid colour. Little by little, too, these cool dark lower floors accommodate shops.

In the centre of the town stands the coloured Baroque town hall, rivalling that of Astorga in a sort of merry unconcern with serious architecture—a Sancho Panza among town halls, sagacious and absurd in countenance. One remembers here a comment by an eminent English architect upon the new town hall at Stockholm, to the effect that a civic building should not aspire to be a place of all the arts, satisfying the eye at all points, but should be a Petit Trianon, complete, taken in at a glance, of no more ornate planning than serves its immediate purpose. Here then, no bigger than its shoes or its affairs, stands the town hall of Pamplona—

housing the relics of Sarasate, her most famous modern son, looking (perhaps by suggestion) like the royal box at an opera, and filling the end of a plaza with entertainment.

Serious and noble, beautiful in internal symmetry, is the late pointed Gothic cathedral. That it once housed a large college of priests may account in some degree for the richness of its collected buildings, and few cathedrals show so advantageously in these as that of this capital of Navarre. The 'pagan front' is only the imprint of the passing of a mode, its dullness redeemed somewhat by the excellence of its stone (about the date of Worcester College, Oxford).

Renaissance ironwork as fine and of the same date as that in Cuenca encloses the choir, its seats carved of English oak by a workman of Pamplona, and an earlier Gothic *reja*, a triumph of Basque forges, screens the sanctuary with its treasure of the silversmith's work, the statue of the Virgin within its shrine. But among the elaborate gilded *retablos*, none pleased me so much as one, a little in the shadow, painted tenderly and gravely in the early Flemish manner with scenes of the Passion, and, perhaps less intimate but more austere, that of the prophets.

The collegiate buildings, which might at this date have been very bad, have succeeded in being triumphantly good. Among the beautiful cloisters of Spain surely that of Pamplona must rank among the first—its height and grace so pleasing, its ornament and sculpture of such good date, its chapels and gateways charmingly contrived (the ancient washing-place, fenced in now by a *reja* forged, it is said, from chains of Moorish captives, being so notably managed) —the tracery of its windows so graceful, the sculpture so rich. An unusual and delightful enrichment of the cloister arcade is carried in a series of slender gables, above the window traceries, each surmounted by a delicate finial statue. The collegiate apartments, planned for those who live in common, are of the finest. A spacious and lofty refectory was served from a great kitchen after the pattern of Glaston-bury with its central chimney. Gaunt and clean, this apart-ment, rare of its kind in Spain, shelters now the lovely tomb of Charles the Noble and Leonora, King and Queen of Navarre. The triple cross of silver and blue enamel which was given by a Byzantine emperor to this king and by him to the cathedral stands in the treasury, with the silver Gothic sepulchre given by St. Louis, and the rare and exquisite Persian ivory casket which bears the name of Almanzor on its lid.

The fine chapter-house, having outlived all siege and bom-bardment, stands upon the wall, venerable and rigid, like an old tradition among modern ease of manners—its crocketed finials wearing grey, its roof barnacled like the hull of an old sea-weary ship. Its light and graceful loggia, its delicate window tracery, the outstretched throat of the wolf in its gargoyle set high on a building slender and spare as a tower, down which, to the very walls of the ramparts, the buttresses, set cornerwise to an octagonal dome, carry lines of interest and strength, make an imposing silhouette.

The door which admits from the street stands open. Instead of an apartment is disclosed the cobbled pavement of a long obscure stable, dimly enough lit by lamps on either side of a noble staircase ascending to some floor above. Its end cannot be seen from the street. Beneath it, fastened by the bridle, stands a saddle-horse, waiting for whatever refugee, monarch, messenger, is coming down the staircase, to ride off into the night. (It is probably, in fact, a farmer who had business with the house.) But since it is a picture which will soon disappear from the town houses of Spain, whose dim cool stables on the ground floor are slowly being used for shops and storage vaults, I like to think that I have seen it much as Cervantes saw it—the stable under the grand staircase ascending out of sight, and the waiting horse standing in the shadow.

The new quarter of Pamplona, large and airy, shows an interesting development of modern architecture. The planning of the streets is after the manner of the Rambla at Barcelona, and the buildings have escaped that air of the Paris Exhibition which clings to the modern quarters of some old Spanish towns. The architects are to be congratulated on much that is being done, and upon ornamental experiments in the synthetic materials used for shops and garages. There is a modern monument by Benlliure in the cemetery; for if one is setting out to be modern, why, indeed, in these days, not be whole-heartedly so?

Chapter Thirty-two

POPULAR LIFE: I

GRACE O' LIFE

When George Borrow rode out of the 'Trojan Horse' in Valladolid after his conversation with the 'daughter of the prison' he wrote his report.

'I found literature of every sort at the lowest ebb in Valladolid.' I walked past the Inn of the Caballo de Troia and believed him—that most picturesque and amusing Parador! But as I wandered later in a shady and green grove in the public gardens in the old Spanish capital the little tiled building which is an open-air library attracted my notice. Around, on benches under the trees, young workmen were sitting reading. The librarian allowed me to examine the books. An inscription always pleases me, even on a tombstone. Inside the book I read this printed notice.

'The Book to the Reader.

'I have come to you confiding in your culture and I am helpless in your hands. Receive me as a friend and see that on returning me to the book-shelves from which I came out to communicate my spirit to you, I carry a good recollection of your treatment. All who turn my pages will thank you for it and you will deserve the censure of all if you do not respond to the gifts which I offer to your heart and your brain, granting to me your affection and respecting my feebleness.'

As I came out through the garden I paused to read yet another notice.

'The birds and the flowers are the brightest adornment of the gardens. To damage the one or to destroy the other is to injure their highest beauty. Whoever does such deeds does not deserve to be a citizen of a cultured township.'

'Oh, that's the grace o' life. We don't go in much for the grace o' life in Aberdeen', explained a friend.

But the modern wooing of the 'grace of life' in Spain has taken this charming direction.

Since St. John of God used to lay holy books within the gate of Granada that those who saw might read, to the modern day of Seville and Barcelona Exhibitions, many gardens have grown and withered. And now, in the gardens of modern Spain, under trees and among the roses, beside fountains, with the arts keeping watch, the pretty plant of culture has been set in a sunny atmosphere.

Though it was at Valladolid that I first came across an open-air library in a garden, my search for similar graces in other towns has not been ungratified. They have a charming

The Christ, San Feliu, Gerona

Corpus Christi Procession, Barcelona

way at Seville of setting the poet's works beside his monument, in a green chapel of the garden. The poet Bécquer,
romantic and compelling, stands in a bosky circle beneath
the trunk of a central tree whose branches reach from rim to
rim. Three marble ladies for ever are wounded, admire, and
are fair; small white marble bookcases hold his works, and
seats invite the reader. In a newer part of the same gardens
Don Quixote and Sancho Panza guard a little tiled garden
for readers. A spreading tree (how quickly it grows) is
planted in the centre of the octagonal seats, whose separate
tiles are the illustrations to their adventures. Their figures,
mounted and ready, are set opposite one another, each on an
open bookcase with the works of Cervantes inside.

For the famous modern dramatists the Quintero brothers
there is a 'Glorieta', for 'one wind fills the two sails' of these
sons of Seville. The two-sailed ship is displayed breezed by
the wind beside an ornamental water. Along the tiled seats
the record of their works makes a coloured frieze. The little
bookcase of gay ceramic is beside a tinkling fountain, and a
plaque holds the double portraits of these honoured-while-
living brothers.

Salamanca, as a place of learning, has a more ambitious
open-air biblioteca. The three sculptured figures of Gabriel y
Galán (the poet of the lands of Castile) and his two inspira-
tions, Poetry and Rural Beauty, compose part of an architectural whole, of which the kiosk holding the books is the
centre. The Spanish sculptor Cristóbal has managed a happy
conjunction of architecture and sculptured figures gracefully
enough in this pleasant garden of San Agustín.

There were days when gardens and their fancies were enclosed and for the great alone. Sun and roses and soft climates
invite lingering out of doors and the public gardens of

I

Spanish towns grow increasingly beautiful and interesting. It is a happy form into which civic interest is flowing, and the planning of gardens is among the modern living arts. The green enclosures for children in a world many sizes smaller than life are like a fairy-tale for the adult. The grace o' life is becoming prettily at home in many unvisited little towns of Spain.

JERÓNIMO

When the Spanish students wandered with strolling companies of jongleurs and minstrels to earn their university fees, learning went easily, one imagines, where needs were few and a night's lodging could be paid by a song. None the less in these days Spanish students need their fees. One tranquil summer evening, when the offices had all been sung in the cathedral, and the dusky hour before the time of closing was striking long shadows on the floor between the columns, and the angels in the vaulting had their hour of glory, the repetition of a voice still sounded in the silent aisle. Some priest reciting an office? Some penitent? Some devout person freed at last from daily work and offering his release to God? No! Just Jerónimo getting by heart the parts of his anatomy lesson which he needs for to-morrow's examination. For Jerónimo, the son of the sacristan, earns his fees as a medical student by acting as guide to visitors in his spare time. Pluck and resource are delightful qualities which merit pleasing results. Jerónimo had leisure the next evening for conversation. He had got through! 'To-day a guide in the cathedral. On Sunday a *médico* for three days at the Hotel Paris on 20 pesetas a day. On Tuesday back again, a guide in the cathedral.'

EL SERENO

It was midnight in the hotel and we had no stamp for an important English letter. If it were posted over-night it would catch an early post in the morning. The hotel porter had no stamp either. He thrust his head into the street. 'There's the man!' he exclaimed, clapping his hands vigorously. We looked out, curious! '*El hombre! Mire usted!*' he repeated. 'The man' was walking towards us. There was no one else in the street. But were we to go out and accost this figure from the reign of Elizabeth and demand from him a modern fourpenny stamp? It seemed impossible! A man trailing a pike and carrying a lantern and wrapped in a cape to the eyes? Yes! it was the right thing! He hoped we were in good health; laid his pike against the wall, his lantern on the ground, swung his *capa* loose and produced from somewhere beneath it a small tin box. The stamps were within, and with the satisfaction of a man found perfectly efficient he proffered the just amount. The pleasure of two people, each perfectly satisfied with the encounter, warmed five minutes of midnight, and then the Sereno strolled on, his pike in his hand, his lantern round his neck. 'Sereno!' we heard him chant from a distance and wondered what would happen if on any unforeseen occasion he were called upon to use his pike!

DOLORES

It is too bad to tell tales of Dolores, for does she not every morning pat my shoulder with her comely (and strong) hand and offer me sympathy on the hard lot which is mine, to look after and keep in good humour all the men I have with me! She is wonderfully handsome with her straight back and comely shoulders, and has an Oriental regard for a married woman's demeanour.

Now there comes to the hotel a gentleman of great culture, whose Castilian makes the landlord fluent in admiration. One morning, this gentleman, ringing his bell, is confronted by Dolores. Finding she understands nothing he says, he remembers that he has forgotten to put his teeth into his mouth. As he walks over to the washstand and puts in his teeth Dolores understands and completes his request. An hour later he comes downstairs to be greeted by the landlord with convulsions of laughter. Dolores, it appears, has come to him with awe-inspiring news. When first she went into his bedroom the Señor could talk no Spanish at all—then he went over to the washstand and put a little machine in his mouth and immediately began to talk the most beautiful Castilian. Nothing less, it seems, would ever have shaken the self-possession of Dolores.

OUR LADY OF THE SHEPHERDS

As we work on a hillside above the town, a shepherd in a ragged cloak walks round us, leading seven lanky sheep. The sheep nibble the grass between the heather and the shepherd peers inquisitively at our work. Wrapped to the chin in his poor cloak, he never speaks, nor does he answer when we address him. Lean and wild as the hill, at times he raises his head to watch the sky and the clouds on the distant hills. When the rockets which declare a pilgrimage or procession in the town below snap their fires in the air he turns attentive, and the women raise themselves to watch the passage of the fire-balloons which a pilgrimage sends to announce its arrival. The town is so near that but a few steep fields divide it from the hillside, yet up here life goes on, knowing of its affairs only by the sounds which rise from its streets. No one approaches it or is of its ways.

Yet once I saw the shepherd in the town, watchful and still among a crowd waiting for a procession. The figures emerged from the narrow street: the Magdalene in a bower of green; Saint Antony of Egypt; Saint Eulalia; and last a little country Virgin seated beneath an oak with a straw hat and a shepherdess's crook. The child in her arms was like the babies of the country with a straw hat and a posy, and at their feet lay little white lambs, curly and obedient sheep of Our Lady of the Shepherds, for ever white and innocent.

AUGUST IN ASTURIAS

The maize-tassels are ripe. It is time for harvest. 'Scarcely worth the trouble!' say the peasants, grasping ear after flaccid ear. But the crops, shoulder-high and deep enough to submerge the reapers, keep their incessant demands. On long sighs without any apparent wind the rustling of ripeness is sustained all through the shadowed nights. This long breath and the running of the fountain under the wall of the maize field are the only sounds in the dark. The full harvest moon turns the convent buildings to alabaster. High above them is a gigantic stone-pine, perpetually, sombrely, lofty and alone. Anything might happen on those moon-ridden hillsides. The maize-tassels in the field beneath the convent seem to have changed their substance. Now I believe in the gardens of gold and silver which Montezuma's goldsmiths made for eternal blooming. Such an one even now stretches to the last Station of the Cross on the convent wall. The windows of the convent visible above the garden are heavily latticed in the Moorish manner. For some days I have seen a plant hanging from a nail outside one of these lattices. In the evening it disappears. It is put outside then and taken in again. By whom? I am fortunate. I sit on my balcony in the evening and watch. The village people are at their evening meal. Far up in the maize fields the reapers are still singing. The lattice stirs. A thin white hand reaches through the aperture, unhooks the plant and draws it within. In the early morning the thin hand puts it out again into the sunlight. I grow to watch for the hand with the plant. It becomes part of my day and my acquaintance. One day I catch a glimpse of a veil. No more. Romances are made of such things.

Chapter Thirty-three

POPULAR LIFE: II

ILUSION

'*Tenía más arte que suerte!*' said Concepción plaintively. ('He had more art than luck.') And so the five spinster sisters and their mother, whose hearts were always on the verge of tears (often enough for those who never deserved it), gave a room in their hotel and his opportunity to César, whose father had been a friend of their father and who was more gifted than fortunate.

Every day one or other of the sisters sat in an office on the restaurant floor upstairs, one of those inside rooms without daylight common in Spanish hotels. Always dressed in black, their life in the hotel was only varied by visits to the churches. A piety Oriental in its fixity wrapped the soul of the old mother—a widow of five years' length. Never since the death of her husband five years before had she set foot outside the door of her hotel. From her small dark room to the dark office she passed at times, but outside daylight had never touched her since her widowhood. Sometimes she sat alone in the office, on the commemoration of dead relatives, when her daughters went to hear masses, or on days when they went to visit the Stations of the Cross.

They were all good women and charitable, but Concepción was the kindest. It was she who told me how they had seen their opportunity to put fortune and notice within the reach of César. The room which he decorated has become almost a shrine in the middle of the hotel life for these women so preoccupied with their memories of the dead. For, having painted the work of his life, César died. 'How happy he was!' said Concepción. 'What *ilusión!* How he worked, getting books to copy his swans and flowers. With *what ilusión* he painted! He had always more art than luck. Is it not beautifully decorated, this room? He was so happy.' It remains to the five women the most beautiful room in the world, full of the ardour and happiness and '*ilusión*' of the boy to whom they had opened a future.

'If you are obliged to knock a nail in the walls, we should feel it a favour if you would avoid the decorations,' said Concepción a little anxiously.

Be content, kind women. I shall knock no nails in the life of any man: I even find his stiff, untutored pictures pleasing. His lot was not so 'unlucky' after all. To die, having created an ardent belief in his work; to have left the memory of a boy working at last with a fervour of *ilusión*, through their good intervention, is not given to every benefactor to witness.

[244]

THE WOOD-CARVERS

It was dusk as we passed from the last chapel in the Cathedral of Granada, dusk filling a final silence. High in a corner of the spaciousness and gloom of the nave was a lighted space showing like a picture. Across it were hung three pairs of trousers.

'Alonso Cano's studio', said our guide in a matter-of-fact voice. 'And Alonso Cano's trousers?' one blinked. '*Los campaneros*' ('the bell-ringer's'), said the guide. So *that* was how he worked, hidden in one of the numberless rooms which a great cathedral secretes!

A wood-carver's shop is a fine place to visit, even now. The first impression is of the number of men in different attitudes, stooping, lifting, chiselling, hammering, burnishing, at all heights and positions in the centre of a circle of light let down from above into a sort of well of dusk and cobwebs—the workshop less important than the work. Above the humans, thrusting, reaching, and bending, rise the groups of unfinished figures, benign and immobile. The sculptor, high on a ladder, works on a head and arm; seated in the light, a painter with palette and brush gilds the diaper on the Virgin's cloak; little boys sit in corners or stand at benches polishing the wings of angels. The *Maestro* stands, grave, capable, and watchful, in his long smock. Such workshops must have existed for centuries, and the carved wooden figures painted in polychromatic colours are more distinctively Spanish than even the sumptuous blacksmith work of the country; Spanish in origin, in continuance, and in the unchallenged place they hold in the affections of the people. Wherever one sees them one has a pleasure quite otherwise than is given by sculptured stone. Something more intimate has been trying to express itself and succeeds so often because it springs from an unspent interest in the art itself. Its attempts are modest, often done by local carvers for the devotion of humble people (less frequent are the attempts at portraiture)—the *types* are Spanish, in modern work becoming more and more so. I cannot imagine any other country than Spain producing the modern figure of St. Francis, by Asorey. Just as the two figures in the University chapel at Seville by Montañés express that side of the Spanish mentality called 'noble'; calmness, kind and open sincerity of heart, restraint of manner and forbearance of personal intrusion.

In Barcelona one hears now of Christs and Saints manufactured as Ford cars are manufactured—passed on in the gross from process to process. One man paints the eyes, a second the wounds, a third the loin-cloth, etc.

'But how do you dispose of all these images in Spain?'

'Ah! Señora! In Barcelona we are not a pious people! We export them to South America!'

UNLETTERED

The long gallery with its fine row of windows looking across to the Guadarramas, which was once a nobleman's dining-room, is now empty of the farmers and peasants who have finished their midday meal and ridden away over the 'lands'.

Presentación has lifted the table-cloths and swept the floor with her broom of turkey feathers. She has settled to sleep in a corner. A bell rings without any manners, rudely and noisily. Arrivals! In the old days one knew when the trains came and when the diligence set down its passengers, but in these days who knows at what unhallowed times people arrive in motor-cars! Presentación pulls the cord which loosens the latch. Three young men enter quickly, followed by an elderly peasant with a basket. '*Viajeros!*' (travellers) sums up Presentación and asks if they would like something to eat.

They have eaten, it seems, and pushing one of the tables to a window set about their business unceremoniously. Presentación watches them with a kind of patient curiosity as they empty the old peasant's basket of its contents on to the table. It was full of autumn crocuses whose delicate lavender petals now lie drifted in a heap beneath the light.

The old peasant, peering from behind the youths, is more interested than Presentación, for it is *his* basket (not yet restored to him) and *his* labour (not yet paid for). The *viajeros* seem to have forgotten him. He stirs his feet uneasily to remind them that the basket is his. The young men begin with neat and skilful fingers to strip the petals from the saffron of the crocuses. Soon a pile of the ruddy orange pistils lies beside the wilting lavender sheaths. The youths chatter incessantly. The old man gazes intently. This is a new thing. Before he has time to consider it the youths are aware that their supply is not adequate. One of them lifts the basket and looks round for the peasant. Now he may ask for his money. The young men laugh—he must go out and find more crocuses—*many* more, before he is paid. They know he will come back for the money. If they pay him as he demands *now*, he will go away. Juan pushes the basket under his arm, with a hand on his shoulder leads him to the door and facetiously thrusts him outside.

'*Qué muchachos!*' (What boys!) sighs Presentación, and

what are they doing then? She, who has worked from day-break, knows better than call attention to herself, or put her own legs to any useless fatigue. She closes her eyes again. The youths chatter on.

After an interval the old man returns, his basket filled again, the autumn cold coming in with him. Hardly glancing at him Juan reaches his hand for the flowers. The peasant does not now shuffle his feet. Outside he has been thinking. He watches the *muchachos* rifle the saffron from the crocuses. What will they do with it? It is work to which a man could put the children—scouring the country-side for the crocus, and stripping them thus. Paco and María Teresa and Jesús—*they* could do work like that. But what to do with the yellow of the flowers when they were gathered? He does not know. He peers from the shadow of the window, looking intently at the flowers as if to discover for himself. He watches the faces of the *muchachos*. Their work is purely of the fingers for they chatter of the bull-fight in Valladolid. Mystified, he watches. If only he *knew* and could make a profit for himself.

'What's to do?' asks Presentación, wanting the table for supper. Unlettered both, the woman waits to lay the table, the peasant abides the pleasure of the men with knowledge.

THE HANDCUFF KING

The rain of Castile is in earnest. There is no more dalliance about it than there is about the burning of its sun. To-day the plaza is washed as if with a hose-pipe and the cold creeps indoors. In the kitchen of the Fonda three huntsmen are kicking their heels, their dogs with one eye open as if this is too good to be true, lying beside the fire. The inn servant is ironing the trousers of one of the commercial travellers who came in earlier to dry. Until she has finished no meal can be served, for she is using the only table in the room. It is now two o'clock, the rain-smitten plaza is empty with such a definite desertion that the sudden slipping of a shabby two-seater car within its emptiness seems almost a trespass. It is the only moving object in view unless one counts the twanging of long wires of rain in the grey air. The car seems to be of strange shape as it approaches the door of the fonda. Piled with bundles behind, it accommodates two men within. On the step outside holding on to the door and seated with her feet drawn up is a young woman, what remains of her hat cascading water upon her shoulders. Yet when the car draws up she springs to the ground with some sprightliness of manner and tugs at the handle of the door. A middle-aged man with a commercial bag alights and, apparently offering thanks for a lift, enters the hotel.

A young man, lively of aspect, receives his thanks and scrambles from beneath the hood. The girl and he are associates. Leaving the car, the door of the fonda receives them also. Our meal arrives, *after*, and *with* much clattering. Soup of beans and boiled cuttle-fish with large rounds of sweet Castilian bread. At last I have a woman to keep me in countenance at the large table of men. She is very young, half-breed of some kind, and apparently speaking neither English nor Spanish. It is always convenient to suppose that foreigners in Spain are Portuguese, and I am placing their nationality on the western coast when the young man addresses me.

'I am a British subject. British passport. See! Here my passport! British, eh? That's all right.'

The Spaniards are gravely silent while the conversation in an unknown tongue goes forward.

'If you not like what is to eat, they cook you any other thing you want—you like eggs? This my wife. She come with me. Bahamas I come from. British subject. My passport all right.' There is something disarming in the quick black eyes, and the good-natured rather grimy young face. The girl watches him with evident pride.

Our meal is over and he joins us.

'I am illusionist. Come to give show in Sahagún—that is me you see.' He offers us printed papers telling of a show in San Francisco by 'Billy, the Handcuff King'.

'I go now to put these out in the street and see if I get a hall. These people here they never see nothing. You come to my show? Look at this.'

We look. We see a human form escaping by unimaginable contortions from bonds and fetters.

'I go to put these in the windows and get a hall.'

He goes, the handcuff king, and presently returns.

'These people no good. What do you think they do with their hall in the winter? You can't guess? They keep their wine in it! Hall's full of barrels—great casks! They won't take it out. Isn't that a theatre now? Full of barrels and they won't move 'em. I'm going on to next town see if I can get a hall. No good this place. If you want a lift to any place in twenty kilometres I can give you one.'

Not *one* kilometre in that rain, or that car, but we thank him. Later he returns.

'All right. Very good hall next place. To-morrow go on there. They think maybe they'll turn out the barrels from this theatre now. I dunno. Did you ever hear people use their theatre keep wine in? Costs too much to turn it out, they say. But next place is all right.'

As we gather again round the big table for our supper the

handcuff king is paying his bill with alarming altercation. The little half-breed wife stands like a wilted ear of corn beneath the grave and disapproving gaze of the Spaniards. The dueña of the fonda, a large and imposing woman, stands like a Newfoundland before the yapping of a Pekinese. No one could doubt the issue. The handcuff king pays what is asked, aims a Parthian shaft as he tells us that these people need watching about the bill, and with his dejected little wife goes out into the rain and the darkness to the next town.

No one leaves a Spanish fonda without a summing-up. The dueña, having gained her end, can afford to be silent. But the table cannot let it pass. Something is required before dignity is restored. The oldest commercial traveller breaks the silence.

'Those are not English people,' he observes to his *vis-à-vis* across the table.

'They are not English people,' agrees the table with sombre satisfaction, and something of the profound distaste of the populace of Sahagún to disturb the winter sleep of their vintage for the entertainment of the handcuff king booms in their very intonation.

INDEX

INDEX

INDEX

INDEX

INDEX

THE END

OLD SPAIN

DRAWINGS *by* MUIRHEAD BONE
DESCRIPTIONS *by* GERTRUDE BONE

The Edition is limited to 265 copies, in two lavishly illustrated volumes (13¾ in. by 20½ in.), 250 of which are for sale. Bound in brown pig-skin, each set is signed by Author and Artist.

EACH PURCHASER will be supplied with one large and one small Dry-point of Spanish subjects, especially executed for this work by Muirhead Bone. Only 133 of each of these have been printed, and the plates destroyed.

The volumes contain: 120 full-page plates, of which 3 occupy double pages; 34 half-page plates and head-pieces, and 27 tail-pieces, all reproduced in collotype. Many of the drawings are in colour. The descriptive letterpress by Gertrude Bone occupies 260 pages.

Price: One Hundred Guineas

The Connoisseur says:—"This two-volume folio work must surely be awarded pre-eminence among publications of the century. . . . The price asked for *Old Spain* is heavy, but not too heavy when we consider that we shall assuredly never see its like again."

MACMILLAN & CO. LTD., LONDON

BAY OF BI

La Coruña
Betanzos
Santiago de Compostela
GALICIA
Lugo
Právia
Oviedo
Pola de Lena
Navanco
Vijón
Val de Dios
Villaviciosa
Covadonga
San Vicente
de la Barque
Santill
Alta
Ca
Potes
LA LIÉBANA
ASTURIAS
CANTABRIAN
Villafranca
del Bierzo
San Miguel de
Escalada
León
Astorga
Mansilla
Sahagún
Ponferrado
Sanabria
San Pedro de Nave
Bragança
Zamora
Toro
Palencia
Valladolid
C A S T
San Román de Hornija
Medina del Campo
Madrigal
Salamanca
Arévalo
Ávila
Segovia
Eresma R.
SA. DE S. GUADARRAMA
Madrid
Vigo
Braga
Oporto
Lamego
Duero
Coimbra
Ciudad
Rodrigo
SIERRA DE GREDOS
Oropesa
Talavera
Aro
Toledo
Aljubarrota
X
R. Tajo (Tagus)
Cáceres
Trujillo
Guadalupe
EXTREMADURA
Mérida
Lisbon
Badajoz
P O R T U G A L
R. Guadiana
S I E R R A   M O R E
Córdoba
Guadalquivir
Huelva
A N D A L U S I
Seville
Zahara
Mt. San Cristóbal
LA VEGA
Gra
Grazalema
Alhama
SA. NEV.
X
Ronda
Cadiz
Tarifa
Málaga
Gibraltar
Algeciras
STRAIT OF GIBRALTAR